ROMULUS

and

ROMULUS THE GREAT

ROMULUS

by Gore Vidal

The Broadway adaptation

And the original
ROMULUS THE GREAT
by Friedrich Duerrenmatt
Translated by Gerhard Nellhaus

Preface by Gore Vidal

Grove Press, Inc.
New York

Library of Congress Catalog Card Number: 66-15132

First Printing

Manufactured in the United States of America

PREFACE

In our "serious" theatre it is thought parasitic for a writer to adapt the work of another writer to the stage. And even if by rarest chance the parasite should bloom more beautifully than its host the original, the result at best is considered hybrid and not as we think art ought to be: *sui generis*. Yet the Greeks, Romans and Elizabethans were primarily adapters; Shakespeare was the greatest adapter of them all.

But today, although at any given moment our commercial theatre is dominated by journeymen versions of best-selling novels and cynically Americanized European plays, adapting is not thought a proper pursuit for the "creative" writer. Nor has there been much of it amongst the serious. Only Christopher Fry has made a habit of adapting.

Thornton Wilder extracted *The Matchmaker* from an old German play. Arthur Miller once adapted Ibsen. Lillian Hellman once adapted Anouilh. Tennessee Williams (with Donald Windham) dramatized a story of D. H. Lawrence. But none of these adaptations proved to be anything but peripheral to the author's main work. One can hardly imagine a serious playwright saying: "I've got the rights to a wonderful Avery Hopwood farce. It's junk, but I can make something of it . . . ." And then he does indeed make a distinguished play of an undistinguished one. Yet Shakespeare used anything which came to hand; if anyone had a plot he fancied or a character he wanted to explore, he took it. Contemporary European writers are equally serene about adapting. Bertolt Brecht used anything that caught his fancy; whatever glittered, he took magpie-fashion for his own nest: novels, old plays, new plays . . . it made no difference. He was also most generous in acknowledging his sources, though inevitably he was occasionally charged with plagiarism. Gide solemnly brought *Hamlet* to the French. Camus adapted Dostoevski. The list is endless. Why then do serious-minded American writers regard adapting as "uncreative"? I have a theory.

For some fifty years naturalism has dominated our prose and dramatic literature. It is essential to naturalist doctrine that literature to be good must be "true" and to be true it must, finally, be the author's experience worked out literally. Now naturalism has many merits, but in our time most of those merits have become demerits. In the interest of a superficial honesty our plays grow more and more meager in content. It is not thought quite honest to use the imagination . . . assuming the playwright has any . . . nor is it thought truthful to transcend the limits of one's own personal experience of the world which, for a mid-century American playwright, is apt to be limited. The usual writer comes from the middle class and receives a standard (i.e., not good) education; he then goes either into show business or into the Academy: two ghettos where he is not apt to have much traffic with the life of his time. The world he lives in is small and specialized. This can of course be overcome through imagination. But naturalism insists he eschew imagination. Naturalism insists that he write about what he knows; which is to say himself. And himself – any self – is not apt in a small context to be very interesting. The result? Plays about what happened last summer (no, not suddenly, just very slowly) and how much was drunk and how the marriage went wrong and what the wise psychoanalyst said, and so on toward total boredom. Our naturalist playwright feels that he is cheating if he does not write truthfully about his own experiences. Therefore, he must not adapt, for to adapt suggests a lack of confidence in himself, which is all he has. Isn't there a play in me this year? Am I losing my sincerity, my passion, that profound experience of my generation which, to quote a recent commercialite referring to the night's effect upon a heroine, "beats through me like a storm"? So our "serious" writer leaves adapting to the commercialites who are his natural brothers, lacking only his self-love and self-delusion. The commercialites, incidentally, are a jolly crew. They keep the theatre going. They are often splendid craftsmen. Their spur is not vanity, like the "serious," but money. They are true Americans.

But the attitude of our "serious" writers is contagious. For much the same reasons as theirs, I have resisted adapting, even though I am not a naturalist playwright or, for that matter, a true playwright. Primarily, I am a prose writer with axes to grind, and the theatre is a good place to do the grinding in. I prefer comedy to "serious" drama because I believe one can hone the ax sharper on the comedic stone. When the mask is Comedy, the face beneath can be that of a hanging judge and the audience will not be alarmed; they will laugh and in the laughing listen, sometimes to good effect.

In 1959 I started to read the novels and plays of Friedrich Duerrenmatt. I had seen his play *The Visit of the Old Woman* metamorphosed by the Lunts into *The Visit*. I did not like it. But I was drawn to the play's initial conceit. Duerrenmatt's books, though thrillers, turned out to be moral melodramas of a most interesting kind. All in all, he struck me as a potentially good influence, especially on our theatre, which more and more had shrunk to the small, the private and the irrelevant. Here was a writer who was concerned with the idea of justice; he was in the line of Aeschylus and it was plain that the Eumenides were real to him. I wrote a piece about Duerrenmatt for *The Reporter*, noting:

"Love, like a sense of humor, is now claimed by everyone even though Love, like a sense of humor, is rather more rare that not, and to most of us poor muddlers unbearable at full strength. Our literature both popular and serious is drenched with Love, possessed by Love, usually sexual, though *caritas* will do; and if one only had a dollar for every time the word 'compassion' has been used to describe some writer's best quality, one would be rich indeed. In the theatre, where contemporary prejudices and superstitions are traditionally revealed at their most naked, Love has become *deus ex machina.* Our age has chosen its device (Eros crossed by the male and female biological symbols) and in America, at least, all other themes have been forsaken, dashed to bits on Dover Beach.

"But now, like an avalanche in far-off mountains, comes Friedrich Duerrenmatt, a Swiss detective-story writer with a gift for the theatre, to give us a new theme, or rather to remind us of an ancient one: justice. And he has arraigned with wit our Loving time before that tribunal."

A year or so later, Duerrenmatt and I met. I had it in mind that if there was a particular play he would like adapted for our stage I might be interested in doing it. Playwrights are best adapted by other playwrights. Duerrenmatt agreed. He mentioned a work of his called *Romulus der Grosse,* a fantasy concerning the last Roman Emperor, Romulus Augustulus. He fancied it. I was intrigued. I knew the period; in fact, I was writing a novel about one of Romulus's predecessors, the fourth-century Julian Apostate.

German friends were quick to tell me that *Romulus* had failed in Germany, in France, and in an English version produced at the Edinburgh Festival. The commercialites said: "Don't touch it!" Their point was reasonable: if most foreign hits fail in New York, a foreign failure will lay a memorable egg indeed. Undeterred, I read the French version, as well as a literal translation of the German text. Deliberately, I did not read the English adaptation. I liked the play, though it was quite apparent why it had failed. Duerrenmatt had neglected to dramatize his situation. To paraphrase T. S. Eliot, to be effective in the theatre one must simply be very interesting. *Romulus* was interesting in conception but not in execution. It was undramatic. Early on the Emperor's plan is revealed; he then repeats himself for the rest of the play. Nor is this lack of tension the "anti-theatre" of Brecht, whose success with this sort of fable was, often as not, due to an ambivalence toward the emotional involvement of audience and play which, paradoxically, created the very thing he wanted to eliminate: a tension and an involvement which (as much as he might dislike it) is primarily emotional. Though Brecht aimed at *Verfremdung*, he often created its opposite: not estrangement but involvement. In any case, the amount of thinking you can get an audience to do is negligible. But you must hold their attention for two hours if you want them to absorb a single thought or present them with a single unfamiliar attitude. This is done through the emotions. You tell a story. Now the primitive gift of storytelling does not change down the centuries – a truism which makes one sound rather like Somerset Maugham on one of those black days when he realizes that he is not Henry James, but there it is. Despite our love of novelty and this year's delight in the theatre of the absurd (you see, it's this lack of communication thing that makes it impossible for us to relate: me to you or you to them, so it's no good; after all, "broccoli is often blind," as an IBM computer nicely wrote not long ago), the attempt at communication remains the only reason for writing and, all in all, I suspect we communicate quite as much as sublunar flesh will bear, and that is why literature survives remarkably unchanged in its essentials. As for fashion in America, it seldom lasts more than three years. Where are the Beats today?

But Duerrenmatt is not Brechtian. He is very much his own kind of writer, in form more traditional than experimental, accepting the fact that Pirandello is now traditional. Duerrenmatt is best, I think, in his conceptions: they are startling and idiosyncratic. It is in the working out of his themes that he is often shaky. In *Romulus* he stated his theme early and repeated it without variation for four scenes. Nothing new was said after the first statement. The last scene between Odoacer, the Gothic invader, and Romulus I found particularly disappointing. Each man disapproves of war. Each resembles the other in a most collusive way. Neither is a realized character. Yet with all these misgivings, I decided to try an adaptation, knowing that if the play were to work at all it would have to be a re-creation. For our theatre one would have to drive the narrative harder, and make characters. The last was hardest. Shaw was not joking when he said he got his characters from Dickens (those characters at least who were not himself). Shakespeare and Dickens have permanently influenced their descendants in English. We demand full human creations in our literature. We insist that the screw be turned as tight as the character will bear, and sometimes tighter still.

The writers of the Continent are not like us. Their origins are classic. As Michelet put it, France in the sixteenth century had a choice: either to follow Ronsard the classicist or Rabelais the romantic. France chose Ronsard. Our choice, though less crucial, was between Ben Jonson and Shakespeare. We do.not regret our choice as Michelet regretted Europe's choice. For three centuries our theatre has been Romantic, anticlassical and unintellectual. Recently one thoughtful British critic wrote that with the death of Jonson the intellectuals abandoned the English theatre and never returned. But on the Continent the classical tradition survives; and despite those limitations Michelet deplored, classicism is capable of new variations. More to the point, that tradition has made it possible for almost every important French literary figure within the last century to use the theatre. It is different with us, to understate the matter.

Duerrenmatt is in the Ronsard tradition. He does not give us characters as we are used to them. He indulges in *l'exagération juste*. He gives us argument, humors, paradoxes. In certain plays absence of "character" is not fatal. Brecht could be effective with mere voices arguing point counterpoint; yet when he made Galileo he was in Shakespeare country. He made a full creature. *Romulus* lacked characters and it needed at least two: Odoacer and Romulus. I set to work to flesh out the argument. I brooded over Romulus' past. Who was he to begin with? Why did he embark upon his moral experiment? I made him a former professor of history, an absolutist who saw an old world crumbling and decided to end it neatly (impossibly), all at once, as a moral example. The next problem was to make a first scene which would set the tone without giving away the entire argument. It was a most difficult thing to make. From the beginning, the audience had to be alert to the irony. The jokes are nervous; they are not meant to be epigrams; they tend to go sour for they are the expression of a man whose lifework is about to succeed or fail in a matter of hours. No one must stop him; he must disarm, evade, delay. Yet I gave as many clues as I could. I even tried to explain some of the ironies, for if there is one thing our countrymen lack – blessed as we are with every other virtue and subtlety – it is the sense of irony. The next problem was the final scene. The two men meet: the new world and the old world. Duerrenmatt got it over with in a few pages. Odoacer sits; Romulus stands; Romulus sits; Odoacer stands; they both sit. There is unanimity from the beginning. I tried to make them more unexpected: two men of a quality but in a duel.

From the first performances audiences accepted what I was most afraid they would reject: the abrupt shifts from humor to seriousness, wit to tragedy. Both the serious and the commercialites assured us it could not be done in the American theatre, but the agreeable thing about the theatre is that no one can calculate in advance what will work. The reviews were generally amiable. One criticism of the play I feel called upon to correct was that of a weekly reviewer who thought we were saying that all international matters might be settled if two nice men sat down together and had a chat. Neither Duerrenmatt nor I meant any such thing. The note struck – again – was ironic. Marooned in the present, the two men decide to live as long as they can and as well as they can, each profoundly aware of the tragedy to come but in the ironic spirit "we shall as sovereigns *act* as though all the accounts in the world have been finally settled, as though spirit has finally triumphed over matter." The operative word is "act." The statement ironic. They are interested, finally, in "moral experiment not political demonstration."

Plays like *Romulus* have a difficult time on Broadway. The

characters wear sheets. References are sometimes made to unfamiliar names like Plato. Two generations of naturalism have accustomed our audiences to being flattered in the theatre. They want to see themselves in a nice light, and themselves not then but now. They will go to *J.B.* as they might go to church, to be bored in a worthy fashion. Other periods tend to mystify and bore. Also, wit, irony, satire tend to make us uneasy. Outright vituperation like that of John Osborne is perfectly acceptable. He can be laughed at for his rage. But should the audience suspect that *they* are being laughed at from the stage, the result can be disagreeable. I used to listen to the odd laughter at *Romulus*. It would begin after a line the audience thought funny; then it would die in the throat and there would be a half gasp . . . what *are* they saying? Can it be that we are not loved in this house, but judged? I put the case rather more strongly than the play warrants. *Romulus* was more good-humored than not. I did get the impression in some quarters that no play of intellectual worth should cheapen itself by making topical references, that to be serious is to be solemn. I think not, though God knows, a ponderous elevation of tone does seem to suit the American temperament, as play after play demanding attention be paid it continually demonstrates. But "true comedy," as Voltaire observed, "is the speaking picture of the follies and foibles of a nation." True comedy uses everything. It is sharp; it is topical; it does not worry about its own dignity; it merely mocks the false dignity of others. Aristophanes did not write to be great in eternity. He wrote to influence the life of his day. He used every kind of joke he could think of, and many of them concerned people sitting in his own audience, references often unfathomable to us now. But Aristophanes endures because of his engagement in the vulgar life of his time. *Romulus* in its way is equally a speaking picture of some of our day's follies and foibles. I hope its less than glorious fate will not deter others from trying the same sort of play.

I noticed with some amusement that a few unfriendly critics, writing long after the fact, declared Duerrenmatt to be a playwright of dark majesty while I am merely frivolous. In fact, one writer went so far as to say that he had read the German text in order to cite specific examples of how I had betrayed this somber, fine play. All of his examples were inaccurate, the result, I suppose, of a fragile grasp of German. But to set the record straight, here – along with my adaptation – is a literal translation of Duerrenmatt's original play, for purposes of comparison.

G.V.

ROMULUS

by Gore Vidal

The first of seventy New York performances of *Romulus* took place at the Music Box Theatre, January 10, 1962. The play was directed by Joseph Anthony; the set was designed by Oliver Smith; the costumes were created by Lucinda Ballard. Roger L. Stevens produced the play in association with Henry Guettel. Associate producers were Lyn Austin and Victor Samrock. The original cast was as follows:

ROMULUS AUGUSTUS	Cyril Ritchard
JULIA	Cathleen Nesbitt
REA	Suzanne Osborne
ZENO	Earl Montgomery
AEMILIAN	Ted van Griethuysen
METELLUS	George S. Irving
TULLIUS	William Le Massena
TITUS	James Olson
ACHILLES	Russell Collins
PYRAMUS	Francis Compton
APOLLONIUS	Graham Jarvis
OTTO RUPF	Fred Stewart
OTTAKER	Howard Da Silva
THEODORIC	Edwin Sherin
CHEF	Dolph Sweet
GOTHS	Allan Miller, Michael O'Reilly, Harvey Vincent, Drew Elliott

Act One: The morning of March 15, 476 A.D.

Act Two: Scene 1: Afternoon of the same day.
Scene 2: Midnight.

Act Three: Morning, March 16, 476 A.D.

Setting: Audience room in the villa of the Emperor Romulus at Tivoli, near Rome.

ACT ONE

The curtain rises on the audience chamber and garden of the Emperor's villa. The audience chamber should be airy, nonrealistic, blending on three sides with a tangled garden of ilex trees and rose bushes gone wild. Upstage a great bronze door opens into the main part of the villa. On the upstage wall is a pediment supporting a dozen busts of past Emperors. The farthest bust, at stage right, is of the first Romulus, a choleric-looking man whose eyes are tight shut as though he cannot bear to see what is happening. Above the pediment, directly over the door, is a huge Roman eagle. It seems a respectable Imperial eagle until one notices that most of its tail feathers are missing and that the head, instead of glaring off to the right, is turned anxiously to the left, as though fearing an attack from the rear. Beneath the eagle in tall letters upon marble is the legend: SPQR. Downstage center is an outdoor terrace, a step lower than the room. Here a table and two chairs are set. The audience chamber is almost bare with tall arched windows. At stage right, a throne is set against the wall. Against the upstage wall there is a small table on which rests a huge visitor's book, open. Downstage left and right are two tubs of flowers.

As the curtain rises, the stage is empty. The silence is broken by a shout: "Hello!"

Then Titus, *a young Roman officer in uniform, dusty, weary, his tunic stained with blood, staggers into view from stage left. He pauses downstage, to get his breath. He looks about him. He puts his head inside the audience chamber.*

TITUS. Hello! (*Off.*) Hey! Hey? Anybody home?

(TITUS *crosses to the great room. He steps into it. At that moment the bronze door opens and two ancient courtiers enter,* PYRAMUS *and* ACHILLES. *They move slowly, ceremoniously. One carries the Emperor's cloak. They are obviously performing ritual tasks through this scene. They ignore* TITUS.)

Thank God! I was afraid nobody was here.

(*Deep breath.*)

I come from Pavia!

PYRAMUS (*drily*). That is your misfortune.

TITUS. No, I mean I come from the army at Pavia, from General Orestes. I have a message for the Emperor!

ACHILLES. Kindly lower your voice. Romulus Augustus, our Divine Emperor ...

(ACHILLES *and* PYRAMUS *bow their heads and genuflect.*)

... is resting.

TITUS. Well ... Wake him up! I have to see him. Here!

(*Pulls forth scroll.*)

News from the front. *Urgent* news.

PYRAMUS. Have you an appointment?

TITUS. How could I have an appointment? I come from Pavia ...

(*From stage left,* ACHILLES *rolls a breakfast tray into view.*)

ACHILLES. He seems obsessed with Pavia.

PYRAMUS. Do you have a name?

TITUS. Titus, Prefect of Cavalry.

ACHILLES. Then sign the visitors' book.

(*He indicates book upstage.* TITUS *crosses to it.*)

PYRAMUS. Your full name ...

(TITUS *writes indignantly.*)

ACHILLES. Military rank ...

PYRAMUS. Place of birth ...

ACHILLES. Ambition in life ...

(TITUS *flings down the pen in disgust.*)

TITUS. In the name of Heaven, I *must* see the Emperor.

ACHILLES (*reasonably*). If that is your ambition in life, then write it down.

TITUS. Look here, the news I have is urgent! The Roman Empire is on the verge of total collapse.

PYRAMUS. Don't be melodramatic.

ACHILLES. How can that which is eternal end?

PYRAMUS. The Roman Empire is eternal. And therefore – oh, the beauty of classical logic – the Empire cannot end!

TITUS. The Goths are coming. They've broken our defenses.

ACHILLES. For five hundred years the Goths have been on the march to Rome.

PYRAMUS. But they never quite make it to the city.

ACHILLES. Oh, sometimes they get as far as the suburbs. Then they lose interest.

PYRAMUS. I can't think why.

TITUS. Listen, you two ...

ACHILLES. Careful! We are hereditary Lords of the Bedchamber ...

TITUS (*pleading*). Then please, Lords of the Bedchamber ...

PYRAMUS. Most Serene and Illustrious Lords of the Bedchamber is the actual form of address ...

TITUS. Oh, God!

(TITUS *turns away*. PYRAMUS *takes pity; he crosses to him.*)

PYRAMUS. Now ... now, my boy, a career at court cannot be made in a day. You have made a bad first impression – that's true – but don't give up. (*Looks at watch.*) In two hours, at ten o'clock sharp the Lord Chamberlain will arrive at his office, that's in the annex ... (*Points stage right.*) ... across the garden. Write your name in his book, requesting permission for an audience with the Master of the Sacred Household. Then present yourself to him, and I predict that you will be received by our Divine Emperor in less than three days' time.

(TITUS *is defeated.*)

TITUS. Unhappy country whose fate depends on two damned dithering idiots!

(TITUS *runs off through the garden stage right.* PYRAMUS *and* ACHILLES *look at one another thoughtfully.*)

PYRAMUS. I don't think that young man will be a great success at court.

ACHILLES. I'm afraid he lacks ...

PYRAMUS. Tone.

ACHILLES. It is curious that as an empire declines there is a noticeable ... ah, *how* shall I put it?

PYRAMUS. Succinctly.

ACHILLES. A noticeable *decline* in manners ...

PYRAMUS. As well as in values. And if I may say so, he who fails to recognize the value of civilization ... that is to say, the value of you and me, digs the grave of Rome.

(ROMULUS AUGUSTUS *enters. He wears a toga; in his hand, he carries the imperial wreath, reduced now to a circlet with only seven gold leaves. Idly, he scratches his back with it.* PYRAMUS *and* ACHILLES *salute and then fall face to the floor, all beautifully executed.*)

PYRAMUS AND ACHILLES. Hail Caesar!

ROMULUS (*sleepily*). Hail!

PYRAMUS. Great is Caesar!

ACHILLES. Magnanimous!

PYRAMUS. Divine!

ACHILLES. All powerful!

PYRAMUS. All wise, Caesar!

ROMULUS. You exaggerate. Is today the Ides of March?

PYRAMUS. Yes, Caesar. Today is the Ides of March.

ROMULUS. Then we must watch our step.

ACHILLES. The day according to law ...

PYRAMUS. And sacred precept ...

ROMULUS. ... that all government officials are to be paid. An old superstition. To prevent the Emperor from being murdered. Call the Treasurer. Warn him that it's payday.

(ACHILLES *and* PYRAMUS *help him into his robe.*)

ACHILLES. The Treasurer has fled, Divine Caesar.

ROMULUS. Fled? Why?

ACHILLES. He hoped by fleeing to conceal the bankruptcy of the Roman Empire.

ROMULUS. That was clever. He who would cover up a great scandal had best create a small one. Pyramus, make a note of what I just said. Posterity will be amused. Where is the Treasurer now?

(PYRAMUS *removes a small notebook, and writes in it. He will often in the course of the play record* ROMULUS' *asides.*)

PYRAMUS. He has taken a position as salesman with a firm in Syracuse. They sell string.

ACHILLES. He is on what I believe is vulgarly called a "commission basis."

ROMULUS. *Against* a regular salary?

PYRAMUS. Yes.

ROMULUS. Fortunate man!

ACHILLES (*horrified*). But he is in ... in ... ah, I cannot say the word!

PYRAMUS. I can. He is in *trade*. He can never be received at court again.

ROMULUS. Pyramus, don't be such a snob. After all, I was a professor of history before I married our beloved Empress.

PYRAMUS. You were a great historian, Caesar.

ROMULUS. Until one morning on my way to class I said to myself, why should I teach history when I might become Emperor and *make* history.

ACHILLES. You are history, Caesar.

ROMULUS (*serenely*). I know. I am the envy of every faculty room in Europe. I am what I used to teach. At times I feel almost mythical. Now, to cover immediate expenses, take this ...

(ROMULUS *removes wreath and breaks off two leaves.*)

One solid 14-carat gold leaf for each of you. Convert them into money, deduct your salaries, and bring me the change.

PYRAMUS AND ACHILLES. Such is the will of Caesar!

ROMULUS (*looks at wreath*). How sad! When I took on this job there were thirty-six leaves on this golden wreath, this outward and visible sign of my solvency. Now there are only five. We shall soon be flat broke.

(*To* PYRAMUS.)

Breakfast!

(ACHILLES *arranges chair and table downstage.* ROMULUS *glances at the visitors' book.*)

I see we had a caller this morning. Rather early, too.

ACHILLES. A young alarmist. He believes we are in serious danger!

ROMULUS (*thoughtfully*). Does he, indeed? So now it begins. We must not lose our nerve. We are at the razor's edge. Gentlemen, today of all days we wear the mask of comedy. (*Beckons to them.*)

PYRAMUS and ACHILLES. Comedy.

ROMULUS. We must prepare for the unexpected and the bizarre. What is serious we shall make light of. What is frivolous we shall attend with undue solemnity. Gentlemen, be alert. Take your cue from me.

(*The* CHEF *enters with breakfast tray.*)

Ah, that looks good. And *three* eggs. What a treat!

(ROMULUS *sits, breaks open first egg.*)

Did my hen Augustus lay this?

PYRAMUS. No, Divine Caesar.

ROMULUS. Tiberius?

PYRAMUS. No, Divine Caesar.

ROMULUS. One of the Claudio-Julian Emperors?

PYRAMUS. No, Divine Caesar.

ROMULUS. Not a Claudio-Julian. Let me think now. Oh, I know, I know. Constantine.

PYRAMUS. Alas, no!

ROMULUS. All right, I give up. Who laid this egg?

PYRAMUS. Marcus Aurelius.

ROMULUS. Such a reliable chicken. Give her an extra ration of corn and confer upon her the title "Savior of the Fatherland." All the other Emperors are worthless, I'm afraid. Did any of them lay?

PYRAMUS. None of our Emperors, no. Only the Gothic Prince ...

ROMULUS. Ottaker? My competition.

PYRAMUS (*nervously*). I'm afraid so, Divine Caesar.

(ROMULUS *goes upstage to a bench where gardening gloves and watering can are set.*)

ROMULUS (*muses*). So Ottaker the Butcher laid an egg.

(*He puts on the gloves.*)

PYRAMUS. *Two* eggs, to be absolutely precise. Oh, I know this is terrible news, sir!

ROMULUS. No, no, no. I am hardened to adversity. And my General of the Armies?

(*He picks up the watering can.*)

PYRAMUS. Great Orestes has laid nothing.

(ROMULUS *comes downstage right to the first tub of plants.*)

ROMULUS. A dud. And my namesake, Romulus?

PYRAMUS. A hen of exquisite proportion, delicious shape, radiant intelligence ...

(ROMULUS *waters the plants.*)

ROMULUS. She is a dear hen. But has she laid an egg?

ACHILLES. Almost, Divine Caesar.

ROMULUS. Almost? I believe that is technically impossible. Either a hen lays an egg or she does not. It is rather like that old Greek joke about virginity: either you are ... or you were ... (*Loses the point.*) or something. I can never remember jokes. Has Romulus laid an egg?

ACHILLES. Not yet, but –

(ROMULUS *crosses to the stage left tub.*)

ROMULUS (*sternly*). Very well! Those who do not fulfill their functions, in this case the laying of eggs, must be sacrificed to the state. Tell the chef to cook Orestes, Caracalla, and myself.

ACHILLES. Oh, no!

ROMULUS. Oh, I, too, am fit only for the pot. And in future I shall eat the eggs of Ottaker the Butcher.

(ROMULUS *waters the second tub.*)

He is also a fiend. But he lays eggs. We must not allow prejudice to obscure that fact.

(*The* LORD CHAMBERLAIN TULLIUS *crosses garden from stage right. He is distraught, his normal state.*)

TULLIUS. Divine Caesar, Glorious Augustus, Emperor of Rome...

ROMULUS. Good morning, Tullius.

(ROMULUS *puts down watering can and removes gloves.*)

TULLIUS. Caesar: a young prefect, Titus by name, has galloped two days and two nights all the way from Pavia to bring you the news.

(ROMULUS *crosses to breakfast table.*)

ROMULUS. Galloped? All by himself? Without a horse?

TULLIUS. On a horse, Caesar. You knew exactly what I meant.

(ROMULUS *sits at breakfast table.*)

ROMULUS. Yes, but you expressed yourself imprecisely.

(*To* PYRAMUS *and* ACHILLES.)

At all times we must speak perfect Latin. Our ablatives, our subjunctives, our genitives are all that we have left to pass on to future generations. Gentlemen, guard your syntax. It is our legacy to generations unborn.

TULLIUS. The young man is near exhaustion.

ROMULUS. Put him to bed.

TULLIUS. But, Caesar, his report is earth-shaking.

ROMULUS. My dear Lord Chamberlain, reports never shake the earth. Actions sometimes do. Actions which we cannot control, since they have already happened by the time we get the report. Reports merely alarm. That is why it is our policy to discourage bad news. Such is the will of the Senate and the people of Rome. SPQR.

TULLIUS. But, Divine Caesar ...

ROMULUS. You heard me: SPQR. That means I have just made a law. I shall see the young sportsman in a day or two.

TULLIUS. But, Caesar, you *must* ...

ROMULUS (*warningly*). S – P ...

TULLIUS (*as he goes*). He gets worse and worse.

ROMULUS. Gentlemen, where is the Empress?

ACHILLES. She is in conference, Caesar.

ROMULUS. In conference? So early in the morning? Pyramus, is she plotting against me?

PYRAMUS. I'm afraid so, Divine Caesar. The Empress has been plotting against you since seven forty-five this morning.

ROMULUS. Ah, Roman domesticity!

(*Off-stage can be heard a staccato series of "Hails" approaching.*)

ROMULUS. The art dealer.

(APOLLONIUS, *a Greek art dealer, bursts into view. He carries an attaché case. He opens briefcase, removes magnifying glass, stickers, etc. He is all hurry, all business.*)

ROMULUS. I'd given you up for lost. Where were you?

APOLLONIUS. Alexandria! At an auction. Going, going, gone!

ROMULUS. You prefer an auction to presiding over the bankruptcy of the Roman Empire? Where is your sense of proportion?

APOLLONIUS. Now ... now. I'm just a simple art dealer.

ROMULUS. Simple? I happen to know that you had five hundred plaster casts made of the Cicero I sold you.

APOLLONIUS. Well, that was for the Goths. For the high school system they're setting up in the Gothic forests. They insisted. Had no choice.

ROMULUS. High school system? Are the Goths becoming civilized?

APOLLONIUS. Naturally. The whole world wants a classical education. It's the thing. Status. A sign of status. Amo, amas, amat, amamus, amatis, amant.

ROMULUS. Nice. Apollonius, I shall need some money to pay for the decline of the Roman Empire. It's quite costly, declining. You wouldn't think so, but there are so many built-in expenses. At times I can hardly wait for the Fall.

APOLLONIUS (*eagerly*). What have you got? What have you got?

ROMULUS. What have I got? (*Points to busts.*) My predecessors. The busts of all the great Emperors, on sale. A treasure trove!

APOLLONIUS. I'll tell you if you got a treasure trove or not. You don't mind if I take a close look at them. Make sure they aren't fakes ... Ha ha.

ROMULUS. The busts are authentic. But I cannot guarantee all of the originals.

(APOLLONIUS *starts toward busts.*)

APOLLONIUS (*mechanically*). Actually, the demand for busts isn't what it used to be.

ROMULUS. Oh, here we go again.

APOLLONIUS. My customers prefer Gothic handicrafts. Primitive art is the big thing now. Emperors are a drug on the market.

ROMULUS. I wish you had allowed me to say that.

(APOLLONIUS *studies busts during scene.* ROMULUS *continues his breakfast. The* EMPRESS JULIA, *a stern Roman matron, enters from upstage. She approaches* ROMULUS, *who continues to eat.*)

JULIA. Hail, Divine Caesar!

ROMULUS. Hail, Julia, Sovereign Mother of Rome, empress of every heart, beloved, darling wife ...

JULIA. Don't talk with your mouth full!

ROMULUS. I'm sorry, dear.

JULIA. I have heard a rumor.

ROMULUS. I should have been more surprised if you had *not* heard a rumor. Palaces are designed for rumors. Pyramus, bring our beloved Empress a plate and one of Ottaker's eggs.

(PYRAMUS *sets her place.*)

JULIA. I am told that a messenger has arrived from Pavia.

ROMULUS. Have some wine, dear?

JULIA. Well, *what* is the news?

ROMULUS. How should I know? The messenger is asleep.

JULIA. Then ... wake him up!

ROMULUS. Try one of these little rolls. They're delicious.

JULIA (*begins*). Romulus, you forget that I am ...

ROMULUS. Darling, not now. Not before breakfast.

JULIA. I am Hereditary Empress.

ROMULUS. I know, dear. Beloved, adored wife of the *last* Roman Emperor, only ...

JULIA. Don't say that! Don't even hint that you are the last.

ROMULUS. Why not? The last Emperor of Rome will occupy a charming place in history. Oh, not admired, of course, and a bit *triste,* but different! I shall be the subject of monographs.

JULIA. You will be the subject of a Gothic sword if you don't ...

(PRINCESS REA *enters. She is nineteen, much affected by drama school.*)

REA. Hail, Divine Caesar.

ROMULUS. Oh, good morning. Hail, darling.

REA. Father ... Mother ...

JULIA. Rea, your father and I are talking business ...

ROMULUS. Nonsense. We're having an egg. Sit down, Rea.

(REA *joins them at table.*)

REA. Did you sleep well, Father?

ROMULUS. I slept marvelously well. In fact, it's one of the things I do best. What have you been studying, dear?

REA. I'm memorizing Antigone's lament as she goes to her death. It's awfully tragic.

ROMULUS. Remind me to have your professor banished. Tragedy is proper only in a cold climate. Comedy suits our situation better.

JULIA. Comedy? With Rome in jeopardy? With this poor child's fiancé missing in action ...

REA. Mother, please don't talk about Aemilian.

JULIA. Comedy!

ROMULUS. Yes, comedy. He who is last had best laugh, if I may coin a bit of folk wisdom.

(ACHILLES *approaches from upstage door.*)

ACHILLES. Divine Caesar, the Chief of Staff requests audience on a grave matter involving the fate of Rome.

ROMULUS. Audience not granted. I am coining folk wisdom and having breakfast.

JULIA. Achilles, we shall receive the Chief of Staff ...

ROMULUS (*warningly*). Julia!

JULIA. ... in sacred audience.

(ACHILLES *bows and goes.*)

ROMULUS. Nero and Caligula murdered their wives with far less provocation.

JULIA. You are not Nero. Nor Caligula.

REA. Thank Heaven!

ROMULUS. No, don't thank Heaven, dear. Thank *me*.

(*To* JULIA.)

But I must warn you, I get in a bad temper if breakfast is in any way spoiled by business.

(METELLUS, *a boneheaded general in armor, enters, salutes.*)

METELLUS. Hail, Divine Caesar.

ROMULUS. Oh, hail, Metellus.

METELLUS. As Chief of Staff, I insist you see the Prefect Titus at once!

(PYRAMUS *tries to whisper something in* ROMULUS' *ear. He is not successful.*)

ROMULUS. I thought he was asleep.

METELLUS. No soldier can sleep when he knows his country is in danger.

ROMULUS. Ridiculous! If that were so, we would be a nation of insomniacs and quite useless in battle.

(JULIA *rises majestically.*)

Yes, my darling?

JULIA. You will receive Titus the Prefect.

(PYRAMUS *at last gets* ROMULUS' *attention. He is delighted at what he hears.*)

ROMULUS. No! (*To others.*) I have great news. Ottaker ...

METELLUS (*warming up*). The Gothic monster, the Butcher of Pavia ...

ROMULUS. No, not that chap. I mean Ottaker my hen has just laid a third egg. It is a record. Pyramus, grant her the title ...

JULIA. Romulus, the knife is at your throat and you talk of poultry.

ROMULUS. Emperors come and go, but poultry endures forever. In any case, I don't need to see your wide-awake young Prefect. I am Pontifex Maximus. I read the future. I know auguries. My hen Ottaker has laid three eggs. That means our frontier city of Pavia has fallen to the *real* Ottaker ...

PYRAMUS AND ACHILLES. Oh, no!

ROMULUS. Our army is broken.

REA. Father!

JULIA. I don't believe it!

METELLUS. He is right, Madame. (*Apologetically.*) I didn't want to alarm you at breakfast. But Pavia *has* fallen. The army is broken. General Orestes and his entire army have been taken prisoner by the Goths. The Prefect Titus has brought you the last recorded words of General Orestes. Those tragic words are:

ROMULUS "We shall fight as long as a single drop of blood courses through our veins."

METELLUS. How did you know?

ROMULUS. All my generals say that just before they surrender. Metellus, tell the Prefect to go to sleep. That is an Imperial command, to be disobeyed at his peril.

(METELLUS *bows and withdraws.*)

JULIA. Romulus, what are we going to do? This is desperate.

ROMULUS. Well, I suppose I shall have to issue a proclamation of some sort. You know, one of those "Hold fast for hearth and home" things. That's for the soldiers.

JULIA. Soldiers! If we've lost the army at Pavia, there are no soldiers. They've all gone over to the Goths. Collaborators!

ROMULUS. I shall then make Metellus general of the army.

JULIA. But he's an idiot.

ROMULUS. Only an idiot would *want* to take over our army at this point. Then, after that command decision, we shall issue a communique about my health. We shall reassure the people that my blood pressure is normal, my arteries unclogged, that I have never been more fit ...

JULIA (*bitterly*). Yes, a healthy body and an unsound mind.

ROMULUS (*amused*). Julia!

APOLLONIUS. Three gold pieces for the Ovid.

ROMULUS. Four. Ovid was a great poet.

JULIA. Who is that creature?

ROMULUS. Apollonius of Utica. He's an art dealer. He's buying the statuary.

JULIA. But you can't sell them. They are Rome's past.

ROMULUS. Well, Rome's past is up for clearance sale.

JULIA. Those busts, those statues are all that my father the Emperor left behind in this world.

ROMULUS. Not quite all. There is still *you*, my darling.

APOLLONIUS. All right. Four gold pieces.

JULIA. It's worth five.

ROMULUS. Yes, the Empress is right. Make it five.

REA (*resonantly*). I'm sorry. I can bear this tragedy no longer. I'm going to study Antigone. I am going to prepare for the long trip across the Styx to Pluto's dread kingdom. Farewell!

(REA *exits*.)

ROMULUS. Farewell. Now you've upset the child.

JULIA. Think nothing of it. It's her dramatic lessons.

(TULLIUS *enters from right, running*.)

TULLIUS. Hail, Divine Caesar!

ROMULUS. Hail, Tullius. What's wrong now?

TULLIUS. Zeno, the Emperor of Byzantium, begs asylum.

ROMULUS. Zeno? Shouldn't he be safe at home in Constantinople?

TULLIUS. No one is safe in this world!

ROMULUS (*gently*). Tullius – please – let *me* make the generalities.

TULLIUS. I'm sorry, Caesar.

ROMULUS. Where is he now?

TULLIUS. In my office.

ROMULUS. All right. I shall receive him.

(ROMULUS *and* JULIA *go upstage to the thrones*.)

TULLIUS (*calls off-stage*). Emperor of Byzantium! We're ready! Caesar's ready!

ROMULUS (*to* JULIA). What do you suppose Zeno wants?

(*They arrange their robes with the skill of long practice*.)

JULIA. Our assistance, I suppose. He *is* our cousin.

ROMULUS. *Your* cousin. The Byzantines are your side of the family, not mine.

(TULLIUS *bows.* ZENO *appears; he glitters like an ikon.*)

ZENO (*in a voice rich with ceremony*). Hail, I greet you, Imperial Brother, fellow Caesar, twin Augustus.

ROMULUS. Oh, hello, Zeno. I must say you're looking very natty. If I'd known you were coming, I would've worn *my* Emperor's suit.

ZENO (*formally, to* JULIA). I greet you, Imperial Sister, Empress, Sovereign Mother.

JULIA. I greet you, Imperial Brother, Roman Emperor of the East.

(ROMULUS *starts to sit; a look from* JULIA *brings him to his feet again.*)

Lord of Byzantium, Autocrat of Greece.

(JULIA *and* ROMULUS *both sit.*)

ROMULUS. Well, Zeno, what can we do for you?

ZENO. First, I must recite the five thousand verses of supplication.

ROMULUS. Oh, God!

ZENO. The ceremony of the Byzantine Court is not only a reflection of the world order, it is order itself.

JULIA. How true!

ROMULUS. How interesting.

(ZENO *crosses to them and prostrates himself.*)

ZENO. Great King, help! Oh moon of the dark night of this falling universe, help, *help,* I beseech thee ...

(ZENO *throws himself at* ROMULUS' *feet.*)

ROMULUS. Help granted! (*Takes* ZENO's *hand.*) Congratulations, Zeno, you've done it again.

ZENO (*getting up*). I must apologize for my voice.

JULIA. You have never been in better voice.

ROMULUS. Do sit down. Coffee?

ZENO (*sits*). Yes. Please.

ROMULUS. Julia, darling?

(*To* PYRAMUS.)

Three.

(*To* ZENO.)

How good to see you again.

ZENO. I must say, Romulus, you're a brick to be so nice.

ROMULUS. But why shouldn't I be nice? You are Julia's cousin.

ZENO. Even so, we've been at war for seven years.

ROMULUS. At war?

ZENO. But now we must close our ranks against the Goths, the international menace of Gothic-ism.

JULIA. We must, indeed.

ROMULUS. Have we really been at war for seven years? You and I?

ZENO. Of course.

ROMULUS. Why did no one tell me?

JULIA. We did our best, but you would never listen.

ROMULUS. What was our war about this time?

ZENO. I took Dalmatia from you.

ROMULUS. Oh? Was Dalmatia mine?

JULIA. Of course it was ours. Dalmatia was my favorite province. Father loved it, too.

ZENO. It is nice, isn't it? Anyway, there Dalmatia was, just sitting there, so I took it. I don't know what got into me. I couldn't be more sorry. If you like, you can have it back. Any time.

ROMULUS. Oh, no, my dear fellow. You keep it. I've got quite enough to do right here, around the house. I must confess, Zeno, just between us Emperors I've been rather out of touch lately. People don't tell me things any more. And of course, I've got my hands full, looking after the chickens. Anyway: *why* did you have to leave Constantinople? Naturally, if you'd rather not talk about it ...

ZENO. Oh, no, no. Quite all right. My mother-in-law Verina ...

JULIA. Charming woman!

ZENO. ... made a secret alliance with the Goths and together they drove me out.

JULIA. She was always so energetic.

ROMULUS. But I thought you were *pro*-Gothic.

ZENO (*shocked*). Romulus!

JULIA. He has no tact. The point is that you are *anti*-Gothic now.

ZENO. Exactly. And what we must face now is our common danger. Either we hang together or we hang separately.

ROMULUS (*startled*). What?

ZENO. Either we hang together or we hang separately.

ROMULUS. I thought that's what you said. Is it yours?

ZENO (*complacently*). Yes. Thank you. It's from one of my speeches during the fourteenth Persian War. It's been much quoted.

ROMULUS. I shouldn't wonder. (*Mutters.*) Hang together ... hang separately. *Very good.*

(APOLLONIUS *crosses downstage.*)

APOLLONIUS. For the two Gracchi, Pompey, Africanus and Cato, seven gold pieces, eight sesterces.

ROMULUS. Eight gold pieces.

JULIA. Nine. Not a penny less.

APOLLONIUS. Eight and a half.

ROMULUS. Eight and three-quarters.

JULIA. Nine!

APOLLONIUS. Okay. But I take Marius and Sulla, too.

(APOLLONIUS *goes back to his ladder.*)

JULIA. Romulus, that junk dealer is a cheat.

ROMULUS (*amused*). Junk? You call our classical heritage junk? Really! Anyway, we need Apollonius more than he needs us. We must have money to pay our debts. I insist on settling every account before the end.

JULIA. The end?

ROMULUS (*quickly*). The end of the month.

ZENO. Apparently I am the only one here who is fully aware of the international menace of Gothic-ism.

JULIA. No, I am. Every day I plead with him to take things seriously, to make plans. Zeno, you must help me convince him that the end of the world is not a laughing matter, but bitter.

ZENO. I'll do my best. (*Solemnly.*) Romulus, the Goths are winning.

ROMULUS. Yes, even I am aware of that.

ZENO. Now: *Why* are they winning?

JULIA. Because we have no one to lead us. Because we have an Emperor who is indolent, and facetious.

ROMULUS. Darling, do let Zeno answer his own questions. People always like to answer their own questions, otherwise they wouldn't ask them.

ZENO. Thank you. We are losing because we don't have a proper slogan.

ROMULUS (*surprised*). Slogan?

ZENO. Yes. The Goths are doing quite well with "Progress and Slavery." So I would suggest ... oh, I know you may think me old-fashioned, but I'd suggest, "For Slavery and God."

ROMULUS. Catchy. But I'm not so sure God is on our side these days. I rather think there is an agonizing reappraisal going on.

JULIA. What about "Right versus Wrong"?

ROMULUS. A bit too simple. Besides, they could use it, too. No. I prefer something more practical in the way of a slogan, something ... constructive. Like "For Better Agriculture, Better Poultry!"

JULIA. Don't be a smart aleck.

ZENO. We are also losing because we no longer believe in the Roman Way of Life. Unless we pull ourselves together and believe absolutely and totally in our manifest destiny, we shall fail.

JULIA. Hear, hear!

ROMULUS. Very well, then. Let us believe.

ZENO. What?

ROMULUS (*reasonably*). You suggest that we must believe in the Roman Way. All right, I'm willing to give it a try. So let us believe. Ready? Set? Now: all together: Believe!

(*A moment of silence.*)

ZENO. You're believing, aren't you?

ROMULUS. Yes, I'm believing.

ZENO. Especially in our ancient greatness?

ROMULUS. Particularly in that.

ZENO. And you ... you believe in our manifest destiny to rule the world?

ROMULUS (*ticks them off*). Manifest destiny ... rule the world ... right.

ZENO. And you, Empress?

JULIA. I have always believed in the Roman Way.

ZENO. It's a marvelous feeling, isn't it? All this belief! You can't help feeling that something's happening, right now, with us really believing in ourselves. At last!

JULIA (*blissfully*). At last. Belief.

ROMULUS. And now what?

ZENO. What do you mean "and now what?"

ROMULUS. Well, since we all believe ...

ZENO. Then that's it. That's all there is.

ROMULUS. But what exactly are we to *do*?

ZENO. The petty details can be left to others. We have faith.

ROMULUS. But don't you think that now we are in this ... extraordinary frame of mind, we ought to do something? You know, like save the Roman Empire?

JULIA (*rises*). Zeno, it's worked. He believes.

ZENO. Salvation will now happen quite naturally of its own accord.

(METELLUS *rushes in from right.*)

METELLUS. Caesar, the Goths are marching on the city of Rome!

ZENO. Marching on Rome?

JULIA. Marching on Rome?

METELLUS. I have ordered every man to hold fast.

JULIA. Any man who runs away will be executed. That is an order.

ZENO. When's the next ship for Alexandria?

ROMULUS. Eight-thirty, I think. There's a timetable on my desk. But won't it be awfully hot in Africa this time of year? Especially in those clothes.

JULIA (*fiercely*). Romulus, the Goths are at our gates. Do something. *Anything!*

ROMULUS (*swings up to center*). Very well, I *shall* do anything. Metellus!

(METELLUS *steps to him.*)

I promote you to General of all the Armies of Rome. In the field, in the barracks, and in flight.

METELLUS. I shall save Rome, Divine Caesar.

ROMULUS. Exactly what I had in mind. You are perceptive.

METELLUS. But I must insist on one thing: total mobilization.

ROMULUS. Total mobiliz – what sort of phrase is that?

METELLUS. I just invented it. It means the entire country must concentrate on nothing but the war effort.

ROMULUS. Oh no. No. I don't like that, even as a matter of style.

ZENO. But the General's right. Only this total ... thing can save our culture from Gothic-ism.

ROMULUS. The idea is completely absurd. Nevertheless, I bow to necessity. For you, General, I shall mobilize totally. And I place at your disposal the palace guard consisting of nine men and twelve officers. They are yours.

METELLUS. But Ottaker has an army of a hundred thousand well trained Gothic troops.

ROMULUS (*gently*). The greater the general, the fewer troops he needs.

METELLUS. Never was a general of Rome so humiliated by his Emperor!

(METELLUS *marches off right.* APOLLONIUS *approaches.*)

JULIA. I shall mobilize the defense of the palace!

APOLLONIUS. All right. I'll give you twenty, I'll give you twenty gold pieces for the lot.

JULIA. Twenty-five.

(JULIA *goes.*)

ROMULUS. Yes, twenty-five.

APOLLONIUS. All right, twenty-five. For you, I'll make it twenty-five. But that's for the whole mess.

ROMULUS. It's a deal. But I want cash. Now.

APOLLONIUS. Okay, okay. But I'm leaving one bust. That one there in the entry, the first Romulus.

ROMULUS. The founder of Rome? But why?

APOLLONIUS. Bad workmanship. If you'll notice, he's starting to crumble.

ROMULUS. How you Greeks love a symbol!

(APOLLONIUS *counts out the gold pieces.*)

ZENO. Who is this fellow?

ROMULUS. Apollonius of Utica, I present the Emperor of Byzantium.

APOLLONIUS. How do you do, sir.

ZENO (*impressed*). Not *the* Apollonius of Apollonius Fine Arts Limited?

APOLLONIUS. That is I.

ZENO. Well ... well ... this is an honor, I must say. I get your catalogs regularly. You buy estates, don't you?

APOLLONIUS (*nods*). And sell them.

(ROMULUS *crosses to upstage closet where he places the money in a strongbox.*)

ZENO. Oh, I know, I know. You must pay a visit to the Island of Patmos, a dear little place which still belongs to me, I think. I have a great many original Greek statues there in the palace ...

(APOLLONIUS *shuts his attaché case, gets his hat.*)

APOLLONIUS. Happy to appraise them for you. At a nominal, nominal charge, of course.

ZENO. I wondered if perhaps you might not be able to make me a small advance, just as a token of ...

APOLLONIUS. Sorry. No advances to royalty. Rule of the house. And now, Divine, Divine Caesar, I got to get going. Don't want the Goths to catch me.

ROMULUS. Certainly ... certainly. I couldn't apologize more, having you here just as everything breaks up. Just one more thing.

(ROMULUS *indicates the eagle on the pediment.*)

How much for the Imperial Eagle?

(JULIA *enters with* PYRAMUS *and* ACHILLES.)

APOLLONIUS. Nothing. It's lost too many feathers.

(PYRAMUS *and* ACHILLES *pick up the throne and start off stage left with it.*)

ROMULUS. So it has. How odd! In fact, that bird seems quite alarmed.

JULIA. Everyone, even the bird is alarmed.

ROMULUS (*aware of what she is doing*). Julia, what are you doing with that throne?

JULIA. It's being shipped to Sicily. It was Father's.

ROMULUS. Why Sicily?

JULIA. Because that is where I intend to set up your government-in-exile.

ROMULUS. Nero and Caligula were right.

APOLLONIUS. Well, I'm off. I'll send my packers round for the busts.

(*To* ZENO.)

Nice to meet you, Emperor.

(*To* ROMULUS.)

Emperor.

(*To* JULIA.)

Madame. See you in Sicily. See you in exile. Got to flee now. Going, going, gone!

(APOLLONIUS *goes stage right through the garden.*)

ZENO. Absolutely nobody, nobody will give me credit. Romulus, we are in an impossible profession.

TULLIUS (*off-stage*). Oh! Oh ...!

ROMULUS. And it gets more impossible every moment.

(TULLIUS *enters.*)

TULLIUS (*excitedly*). Divine Caesar, Hail!

ROMULUS. Hail, Tullius.

TULLIUS. He's here! Otto Rupf is here. Right here, in your palace!

ROMULUS. Why?

TULLIUS. He wrote you a letter, Divine Caesar, asking for an audience.

ROMULUS. You know I don't read letters.

ZENO. Who is Otto Rupf?

JULIA. A true patriot.

TULLIUS (*ecstatically*). A good Roman! And a great human being!

ROMULUS. But unfortunately, he makes pants.

ZENO. He makes *what*?

ROMULUS. A new garment. It's worn about the legs. Sometimes called trousers. It's the latest thing, if you're a Goth.

TULLIUS. Romans wear them, too.

ROMULUS. But not in my presence. It is one of the few things I am firm about. I have never seen this hideous garment, and I pray that I never shall. I regard its inventor, Otto Rupf, as un-Roman. We shall not see him, Tullius.

JULIA. You must.

ROMULUS. Why?

JULIA. Because he is the richest man in the world.

ROMULUS. I fail to see what the one has to do with the other.

JULIA. You will.

(*To* TULLIUS.)

Show him in.

(*To* ROMULUS.)

Money can do anything.

ROMULUS (*blandly*). Can it now? You have become quite a philosopher, Julia, in our declining years. Very well. I shall see Otto Rupf.

TULLIUS. Mr. Rupf! Caesar's ready. Mr. Otto Rupf!

(ROMULUS *sits up*. OTTO RUPF *enters from upstage*. RUPF *is a plump, ovoid businessman wearing rimless spectacles and a peculiar-looking blouse which resembles nothing so much as the coat of a double-breasted suit. At his throat is a garish bit of cloth, suspiciously like a necktie. His trousers, however, have been removed and his shirt-tail falls forlornly to the knees, while his spindly legs are ornamented with garters of the most modern kind. The effect at first should be in the general style of the play; then as the eye absorbs details the anachronisms become more obvious. He carries a Homburg, and his trousers.*)

TULLIUS. Mr. Rupf. *Mr. Otto Rupf!*

ROMULUS (*inadvertently*). Good God! I mean, welcome, Otto Rupf.

RUPF (*firmly*). Emperor.

JULIA (*beaming*). Dear Mr. Rupf, what a nice surprise.

ROMULUS. In the name of the Senate and the People of Rome we extend you greetings. SPQR. *What* are you wearing?

RUPF. More to the point, what am I *not* wearing. I was told it was a rule of your court that no one approach you wearing trousers. So I took my pants off in the lobby.

(RUPF *hands his trousers and hat to* TULLIUS.)

JULIA. Oh, I *am* sorry.

RUPF (*to* JULIA). Well, Empress. I got your letter. And I'm here.

JULIA. Oh, you are good.

ROMULUS. Letter?

JULIA. Generous.

ROMULUS. What letter?

JULIA. Kind.

RUPF (*ignoring the Emperor's questions*). Now I guess you know me, Emperor. Our firm, my family's firm, has been in textiles for over two hundred years. I guess you might say I'm the biggest textile manufacturer in the world.

ROMULUS. I might very well say that. In fact, I *will* say it: You are the biggest textile manufacturer in the world.

RUPF. As a pants manufacturer – that's our big specialty – I am here to tell you that if Rome won't wear pants, Rome will fall. The Goths wear pants. They're conquering the world.

Therefore, pants are the wave of the future.

ROMULUS. I am sure you are right. But I assume you did not come here merely to sell me a pair of trousers.

RUPF. Now then: We have here on the one hand the richest man in the world ...

JULIA. You!

RUPF. Me. And on the other hand, we have the Roman Empire, a complete bust. That's you.

ROMULUS (*serenely*). You have a gift for precise analysis.

RUPF. Now for a while there I was thinking maybe I'd buy your Empire.

ROMULUS (*excited, pleased*). You were? Oh, my dear fellow, we must have a serious talk. Yes indeed, a really serious talk. You were right, Julia, about money.

RUPF (*through him*). No, no. You got me wrong. I'm not going to buy.

ROMULUS. Oh, dear! And for a moment I'd hoped ...

RUPF. No. I decided your Empire's not a good property. It would cost a fortune just to renovate it and even then who knows if you'd ever make a cent of profit. No, I'm against buying, even at sacrifice prices. But I'm not against ... merger.

ROMULUS. Merger? But how do you propose we merge your excellent business with my somewhat ... seedy Empire?

RUPF. Your trouble is you don't think big. You don't think organically. To be a success you got to think organically, step by step. Now, *first* step: Get the Goths out of Italy, that's A-Number-One on the agenda.

ROMULUS. But won't that be a bit difficult? I mean, suppose they don't want to go?

JULIA. Mr. Rupf can do anything.

RUPF. Nothing is difficult when you got ready cash.

JULIA. Oh, you're so right! (*To* ROMULUS.) He's so right.

RUPF. I been in touch with Ottaker. I made him a tentative offer. For ten million he'll go back where he came from. And I got it in writing.

ROMULUS (*startled*). Ottaker?

RUPF. That's right. For ten million, he goes home.

JULIA. You see?

ROMULUS. Odd? I should have thought that he, of all people, would be incorruptible. The whole point to monsters is that they are sincere.

RUPF. Sincere or not, you can buy anybody, Emperor. Just a matter of price.

ROMULUS. You have shattered my last illusion. What do you want from me in exchange for your assistance?

RUPF. I'm willing to pay off Ottaker. I'll even toss a few million into the kitty. You know, just to get the old show going again. But in exchange, everybody, but everybody's *got* to wear pants.

ROMULUS. What else?

RUPF. I marry your daughter Rea. Thereby cementing our merger organically.

ROMULUS (*coldly*). I'm sorry.

JULIA. Romulus!

ROMULUS. My daughter is engaged to be married to a young patrician ...

JULIA. Who has been a Gothic captive for nine years ...

ROMULUS. Captive or not, she loves him ...

JULIA. How could she love him? She was betrothed as a child.

ROMULUS (*to* JULIA). I'm sorry.

(*To* RUPF.)

I'm afraid, Mr. Rupf, we must decline your generous offer and continue with our ... fall.

RUPF (*on his own track*). I hope you got the picture: If you don't merge with a solid firm like mine, your empire's had it and Gothic-ism has won the struggle for men's minds, like they say.

TULLIUS. Yes, yes.

ROMULUS. Good day, Mr. Rupf.

RUPF (*to* JULIA). Well, Empress, looks like you got me here under false pretenses.

JULIA. No, no!

RUPF (*to* ROMULUS). I ought to warn you if I get a turn-down from you I'll marry Ottaker's daughter.

JULIA. Mr. Rupf, you wouldn't – you *couldn't* do that. (*Sotto voce.*) Don't listen to my husband. He's not himself these days.

RUPF. The Rupf firm has got to have an heir. And a Gothic connection makes a whole lot more sense than a Roman one, organically speaking. But I got this sentimental streak.

JULIA (*smiles*). You love our daughter. What could be more natural?

RUPF. The daughter of the Caesars would give a lot of tone to company parties. The big wholesalers are suckers for royalty. Especially the Chinese. That's right, I'm out to land the Chinese account. I think big.

JULIA. You *are* big! That is why you inspire us all.

ROMULUS. Good day, Mr. Rupf.

JULIA (*to* RUPF). Don't go. Tullius, look after Mr. Rupf, while the Emperor and I discuss this happy event.

RUPF. Well, while you're discussing I'd like to look at the books. I want the big over-all organic picture of your empire.

TULLIUS. Only too happy to show you everything.

(TULLIUS *and* RUPF *start off stage right.* ZENO *runs after them.*)

ZENO. Mr. Rupf, I am the Emperor of Byzantium. Have you ever been to the Island of Patmos?

(TULLIUS *and* RUPF *and* ZENO *go.* JULIA *turns to* ROMULUS *who starts to go off through the garden.*)

JULIA. Romulus, come back here. You cannot escape this.

ROMULUS. Escape what?

JULIA. Whether you like it or not, Rea must marry Mr. Rupf.

ROMULUS. I was quite prepared for a nominal sum to sell the Empire to your friend ... and pen pal. But I will not give him my daughter for all ... for all the tea in China.

JULIA. You might not. But think of Rea. She is a patriotic Roman girl. She would sacrifice herself gladly to save Rome.

ROMULUS. But I won't let her.

JULIA. Rea is a small price to pay for Rome.

ROMULUS. As usual, you are so maternal.

JULIA. It is the end of the world if Rea does *not* marry Otto Rupf.

ROMULUS. You mean it is *our* end. Which is not precisely the same thing.

JULIA. We are the world.

ROMULUS. Hardly. We are poor country cousins in a strange new era, where people speak a different language and wear pants.

JULIA. I don't understand you.

ROMULUS. I know you don't.

JULIA. I have never understood you.

ROMULUS. Many happy marriages have been based upon complete mutual misunderstanding.

JULIA. Happy!

ROMULUS. I am given to hyperbole.

JULIA (*gestures at room*). Look at what has become of us! When I was a girl, this shabby room glittered with attendants, courtiers, statesmen. This was the center of the earth, right here, and I was proud, oh, so proud, to be the daughter of Caesar.

ROMULUS. Then after many years of exquisite pride, you married me.

JULIA. Yes. And ever since I have had to watch day by day the world that was ours shrink to this one house ... to dust, cobwebs, empty rooms ...

ROMULUS. Come now, it may be a bit run-down, but it's still home.

JULIA (*furiously*). Why must you always mock us?

ROMULUS (*softly*). I mock what is false. I honor what is true.

JULIA. Well, it is true that Otto Rupf can save us. It is also true that if you try to stop him, others will stop you!

ROMULUS. Is that a threat?

JULIA. That is a threat.

ROMULUS. Be careful, Julia. Be very careful. The comedy is a mask. The face is one you have never seen. If you stand in my way, even *I* may turn monster.

JULIA. Is that a threat?

ROMULUS. That is a threat. You must not interfere.

JULIA. Then what, in the name of Heaven, *do* you plan to do?

ROMULUS. Nothing.

JULIA. I am ashamed to be your wife!

(JULIA *goes.* ROMULUS *calls after her.*)

ROMULUS. But I do have a plan.

(JULIA *laughs derisively as she goes off stage right.*)

ROMULUS (*to himself*). I have always had a plan. From the very beginning. And I must not fail.

(PYRAMUS *and* ACHILLES *enter with pitchers and ewer.*)

ROMULUS. Oh? (*Recalls himself.*) Yes, I am finished.

(*He washes his hands as* TITUS *enters and drops to his knees before him.*)

TITUS. Hail, Caesar!

ROMULUS. Hail. Who are you?

TITUS. Titus, Prefect from the army.

ROMULUS. How do you do?

ACHILLES. This is not polite, young man.

PYRAMUS. This is not done.

(ROMULUS *waves them away.*)

TITUS. For two days and two nights I've ridden. Seven horses died beneath me. I am wounded, yet when I got here they wouldn't let me see you.

ACHILLES. He had no appointment.

(TITUS *draws a scroll from his belt.*)

TITUS. Divine Caesar, here is the last message of your last General as he was taken prisoner by the Goths.

(ROMULUS *takes the scroll.*)

ROMULUS. How extraordinary! Just look at you! Exhausted, wounded ... Why do you put yourself to so much trouble, when you should be in bed?

TITUS. That Rome may live!

ROMULUS. No one has yet found a way to raise the dead.

TITUS. But Rome's not dead. There's still us!

ROMULUS. You? Me? Against all of history? No.

TITUS. But what about my country ... ?

ROMULUS (*softly*). You have no country. Don't you see? Time played a trick on you. You were born too late to change the awful past and born too soon to make a better future. We are in no man's land. (*Rises.*) Get some rest, Prefect.

(ROMULUS *starts off stage right.* TITUS *follows him.*)

TITUS. Caesar, we *must* fight.

(ROMULUS *turns.*)

ROMULUS. Fight? For what?

(ROMULUS *drops the scroll, then goes. A rooster crows.* TITUS, *stunned, turns to* PYRAMUS *and* ACHILLES.)

TITUS. But that *can't* be the Emperor of Rome.

(PYRAMUS *and* ACHILLES *go, without response.*)

TITUS (*slowly*). This is a dream ...

ACT TWO

SCENE I

Later that afternoon. TULLIUS *is working on a bench.* METELLUS *is on another bench, asleep. Smoke billows from stage right.* TITUS *runs in from stage left.*

TITUS. Smoke! Smoke; Hey, what's happening? What's on fire?

TULLIUS. We're burning the archives. The Emperor's orders.
(TITUS *looks at his boot.*)

TITUS. Oh, I stepped on an egg. What a mess! This damned cackling and nobody doing anything ... anything!

TULLIUS. Speak for yourself. *I* am making plans for the government's removal to Sicily. You have no idea what a lot of paper work that involves. And General Metellus there is working on his plan of battle.

TITUS. Plan of battle? He's sound asleep! Everybody's asleep!

TULLIUS. I certainly wish you were.

TITUS (*indicates stage right*). There *couldn't* be an Emperor like that. (*Nervously.*) Could there?

TULLIUS. There could be and there is. He's quite unorthodox in his ways. I suppose that's because he's an intellectual. They say his books are brilliant – especially "The Moral Principle in History." But I couldn't get through it. Of course he's from one of the best families. The Empress had to marry him because – now let me see – though her father was Emperor, her mother was a slave. Yes, that's right. So *only* by marrying a patrician could she become Empress. Oh, I love genealogy!

TITUS. He said I had no country. He's crazy.

TULLIUS. Yes. It's quite possible he is crazy. In fact, if it weren't for the Empress, there wouldn't be an Empire now. She keeps the whole thing going.

TITUS (*suddenly*). Yes! I'm right. This *is* a dream. Look, I can walk through this pillar, through solid stone. See? It isn't real. Nothing's real. (*Crashes into column.*) Ow!

TULLIUS. It's real. Our great hope was Aemilian, a young patrician at court. He was engaged to marry the Princess. Wonderful soldier. We all hoped he would take over one day *but* he's missing in action.

(*A* CHEF *enters with three dead chickens and a knife.*)

CHEF. By Imperial decree the menu for today, the fifteenth of March, 476 A.D. Filet de sole Normande. Poularde aux truffes Romulus. Salade Verte. Bombe glacé Julia. (*To* TITUS.) Will you look at these scrawny chickens? Supposed to be broilers. They are an insult to my talent. An affront to my art. I, who once created thirty-course dinners for sittings of five hundred am now reduced to (*Waves chicken.*) these. The world is ending. My kitchen is cold. My pots, my pans reproach me. I cannot face my stove.

(CHEF *leaves stage right.*)

TULLIUS. He's very good with leftovers.

(METELLUS *stirs on his bench.*)

METELLUS. Shut up.

TULLIUS. You see! You mustn't talk so loud. General Metellus needs his sleep if he's to save us from the Goths.

TITUS. The cackling ... my nerves ...

TULLIUS. Do stop complaining. And stop fidgeting.

(METELLUS *sits up, angrily.*)

METELLUS. Look, I am trying to think. To concentrate. To make a plan of battle, while you keep chattering like a ... (*Picks up his shield.*) Who wrote that on my shield? (*On the shield has been written "Progress and Slavery."*)

TULLIUS. Oh, they've written it all over everything.

METELLUS. Here in my own headquarters, Gothic agents write Gothic slogans on my own shield! Tullius, we are surrounded by spies and traitors!

TULLIUS. I'm afraid so.

METELLUS. I want a complete investigation by the Senate. It's incredible! Un-Roman activities right here in the palace. I've had enough of this coddling of Goths. We must root out all subversives! Prefect, mobilize totally!

TITUS. Yes, sir. But how, sir?

METELLUS. *That* is an order.

TULLIUS. But, General, the big problem at the moment is: How do we get to Sicily?

METELLUS. To Sicily? We shall fight as long as a single drop of blood courses through our veins.

TULLIUS. Of course we will. But *first* we must escape. For the sake of civilization. You see, I've just completed plans for reorganizing the Empire. We have a great deal of social legislation we plan to enact. Medical for the aged, voluntary of course. We also plan to eliminate the graduated income tax *while* increasing military expenditures at the same time! (*Triumphantly.*) Now: how's that for a program?

METELLUS. Civilians!

TULLIUS. But none of these marvelous things can be done if we don't get a boat.

METELLUS. Well, order a three-master.

TULLIUS. We can't afford one. But we can just about swing a secondhand galley, *if* we get a good enough break pricewise. I wish you'd see to that, General. There's one for sale over in Trastevere.

METELLUS. Now I'm a travel agent.

TULLIUS. I'm sorry.

(*Unobserved,* JULIA *appears at the upstage door.*)

METELLUS. I, who might have been a greater general than Julius Caesar, than Alexander the Great ...

(METELLUS *starts to leave when* JULIA*'s voice stops him.*)

JULIA. But you *are* as great a general as Alexander. It is not your fault that the Emperor has given you no support.

METELLUS. Nevertheless, Madame, I shall do my duty. No matter how harsh.

JULIA. Both you and Tullius will do your duty, won't you?

TULLIUS. Naturally, Divine Empress.

(TITUS *drops on his knees before* JULIA.)

TITUS. And so will I! But *what* is our duty, Empress?

JULIA. Our duty is to "persuade" the Emperor that he must allow the Princess to marry Otto Rupf.

TULLIUS. But the Emperor said No. He seemed unusually firm about that.

JULIA (*sweetly*). But we might change his mind, mightn't we?

METELLUS. He's very stubborn, Madame.

JULIA. We can be stubborn, too.

(*To* METELLUS.)

No matter what happens today, will you stand with *me* ... for Rome?

METELLUS. (*Kneels.*) Yes, Madame.

JULIA. (*To* TULLIUS.) And you?

TULLIUS. (*Kneels.*) Yes, Divine Empress.

TITUS. So will I, Empress. I'll kill any traitor you ask me to. Including the Emperor.

JULIA (*gaily*). Oh, dear! I didn't hear that. I did not hear that. (*To* TITUS.) But I admire your spirit, Prefect. You are what we are fighting for. Youth. Be on your guard, gentlemen. We shall save Rome yet.

(JULIA *goes off stage right.*)

METELLUS (*rapturously*). She *is* Rome. Prefect, whatever she asks us to do, we shall do it! But just to be on the safe side, I'll check on that galley.

(METELLUS *goes.*)

TULLIUS (*gloomily*). Well, it looks like a *coup d'état* to me. How I hate them. The files get so mixed up when you murder an Emperor. And then you have to rewrite all the history books again ... Oh, it's going to be total confusion.

(TITUS *sinks down at the foot of a column.*)

TITUS. Well, I'll do anything. Anything she asks me to do ... If only I can keep awake.

(TITUS *dozes. Chickens cackle.* TULLIUS *continues his paper work.* AEMILIAN, *a tattered, worn, exhausted young man, enters. He looks about.*)

AEMILIAN (*softly*). The palace of the Roman Emperor.

TULLIUS (*starts*). Who are you? You're not a Goth, are you?

AEMILIAN. I'm a ghost.

TULLIUS. What do you want?

AEMILIAN. My father.

TULLIUS. His name?

AEMILIAN. The Emperor. He's the father of us all, isn't he?

TULLIUS. Of every patriot. In fact, the word "patriot" derives from "pater," which means ...

AEMILIAN. So I am a patriot. And I have come to my father's house. (*Looks about.*) A filthy farm house. Chickens underfoot. Eggs in every bush, and somewhere an Emperor, taking his morning nap.

TULLIUS. You seem acquainted with court life. However, you must first sign the book. Then I suggest you request audience ...

AEMILIAN. Hello, Tullius.

TULLIUS. How do you know my name?

AEMILIAN. We've been at many parties together, you and I.

TULLIUS. I rather doubt that.

AEMILIAN. Of course it was a long time ago. One world ago, to be exact!

TULLIUS. Where are you from?

AEMILIAN. Reality. I have come from the modern world to this ... charade.

TULLIUS. That means you're a veteran. I recognize the tone. So bitter. What can we do for you?

AEMILIAN. Defeat the Goths, that's what you can do.

TULLIUS. Well, we're working on that right now. Naturally, it's quite a long-range project, battle of men's minds, you know, basically a war of ideas ...

AEMILIAN. I see you can do nothing for me.

TULLIUS. Oh, I grant you there is an element of tragedy in what is happening. And I do feel at times that perhaps a chapter is ending, but not, if I may complete the metaphor, the book itself. We shall win as we have always won. Our higher culture will defeat Gothic-ism.

AEMILIAN (*suddenly*). You like Horace. You write the best prose, both Greek and Latin.

TULLIUS. Naturally. I am a lawyer.

AEMILIAN. I liked Horace. I wrote perfect Latin, perfect Greek.

TULLIUS. Are you a poet?

AEMILIAN. When there was poetry., I was a poet.

TULLIUS. Then write poems again. "Of arms and the man, I sing."

(*Starts to write.*)

AEMILIAN. But where I have been there was no poetry. There was death. I was dead.

(REA *enters from right, declaiming wearily.* TITUS *gets to his feet.*)

REA. "Thebes, and you my father's gods,
And rulers of Thebes, you see me now, the last
Unhappy daughtei of a line of kings,
Your kings, led away to death."

TITUS. There is nothing puts me to sleep faster than the classics.

(TITUS *goes off stage right.* REA *turns, still play-acting, to* AEMILIAN.)

REA. "You will remember what things I suffer, and at what men's hands. Because I would not transgress the laws of Heaven. Come: Let us wait no longer."

(*She takes* AEMILIAN'*s hand as though he were a fellow character. She draws him after her.*)

AEMILIAN (*pause*). Who are you?

REA. Antigone, going to her death.

AEMILIAN. No, I mean who are *you?*

(REA *lets go his hand.*)

REA. I should ask *you* that. You are the stranger.

AEMILIAN. I'm a ghost.

REA. Oh? I'm not at all surprised. The last few days the omens have been dreadful. At Ostia a calf was born two-headed. Toads fell in the rain this morning. And now they say the spirit of Rome was seen last night in the Forum, weeping and covered with ashes. Yes, I am certain you are a ghost. But then, we shall all be ghosts soon enough. I am Rea, "unhappy daughter of a line of kings."

AEMILIAN. Rea! I didn't recognize you. You are beautiful. But I forgot your face.

REA. Have we met before?

AEMILIAN. Yes, when I was alive.

REA. Did you live in Ravenna? Did we play together when we were children?

AEMILIAN. We played together. In Ravenna. We were children.

REA. What is your name?

AEMILIAN. You will see it written in my left hand.

(*He removes a glove from his hand. With his right hand, he lifts the useless left arm and places it between them on the bench.*)

REA. It's horrible ... all scarred. ...

AEMILIAN. Shall I take it back?

(*She covers the hand with her cloak.*)

REA. I can't look.

AEMILIAN. Then you will never know who I am.

(*With great effort,* REA *uncovers the hand.*)

REA. Give me your hand. Your poor, wounded, crippled hand.

(*She takes the hand, mesmerized; abruptly, she lets it go.*)

But *that* is Aemilian's ring.

AEMILIAN (*nods*). The ring of the man you were to marry.

REA. The skin has grown round the ring.

AEMILIAN. The ring has become one with the burnt flesh.

REA. *You* are Aemilian.

AEMILIAN. I was.

REA (*uncertainly*). Are you really a ghost?

AEMILIAN. Touch me.

(REA *puts her hand on his bare arm. She caresses him, at first tentatively.*)

REA. You are warm.

AEMILIAN. So is the fire in hell.

(REA *touches his face, his lips.*)

REA. Aemilian!

(AEMILIAN *starts to draw away.*)

AEMILIAN. But I'm not Aemilian. I'm not what I was.

REA. You're alive.

(REA *holds him to her.*)

AEMILIAN. These scars ...

REA (*fiercely*). ... are my scars. I love them. Every wound is mine, too.

(*She takes his hand and holds it to her lips.*)

I kiss the torn flesh. I make it whole.

(*He wrenches his arm from her.*)

AEMILIAN. Don't! We can't. It's done. Our day is over. Rea, get a knife!

REA. A knife? What for?

AEMILIAN. A woman can fight with a knife as well as a man.

REA. No, no. We mustn't fight any more. We've lost. Our soldiers are all gone.

AEMILIAN. Soldiers are people. People can fight. There are still people in this palace. Women, slaves, children, politicians. Give each a knife.

REA. But that would be foolish. We must surrender to the Goths. We've no choice.

AEMILIAN. I surrendered to the Goths. I had no choice. Well, look at me. Look what they've done to me! Rea, take a knife.

REA. You frighten me.

AEMILIAN. Do you know the word "duty"?

REA. Yes, duty to you.

AEMILIAN. Duty to your country?

REA. Yes.

AEMILIAN. Which duty is stronger? To Rome or to us.

REA. To us.

AEMILIAN. Rea!

REA (*turns away*). Rome. Duty to Rome.

AEMILIAN. You said the words yourself: "Unhappy daughter of a line of kings." Rea, take a knife. Be ready to do your duty.

REA. That was a play. That was tragedy.

AEMILIAN. *This* is tragedy.

REA. No. I won't let it be.

(*She tries to embrace him; he thrusts her away; she nearly falls.*)

AEMILIAN. Take a knife!

(*She stares at him with growing horror.*)

REA. Yes. You *have* come back to me someone else. But I know who you are. Yes ... yes. I know you now.

AEMILIAN (*softly*). The knife.

REA. I see the empty eyes, the dreadful smile. You are what we fear in the night. The shadow at noon. You are death!

(REA *turns abruptly and goes.* AEMILIAN *looks after her a moment; his strength recedes. He puts on the glove he has removed.* TULLIUS *approaches him.*)

TULLIUS (*nervously*). Aemilian, sorry I didn't recognize you, old fellow. Good to have you back. Welcome home.

AEMILIAN. Why aren't you armed? Why aren't you ready for the Goths?

TULLIUS. Now, look: I know you've gone through a lot and we are all terribly, terribly proud of you, but please don't ever think *we've* been having an easy time of it here at the palace, with all the confusion, and the shortages. Especially paper. Do you realize the Emperor is forced to write his decrees on – (*Holds up paper.*) – the back of unpaid bills?

AEMILIAN. Have you ever seen Ottaker?

TULLIUS. The Gothic Butcher? No, fortunately. And I hope I never shall.

AEMILIAN. He is a destroyer. A monster ...

TULLIUS. True, true, in fact, only the other day I was saying: "Ottaker is a monster."

AEMILIAN. He has sworn to murder Rome, to murder you and me. Tullius, at this very moment Ottaker is at ...

(OTTO RUPF *marches in from stage right.*)

RUPF. Gentlemen, your Empire isn't worth a plugged denarius. And the bookkeeping! Worst mess I ever saw.

TULLIUS. Oh, a little untidy, perhaps.

AEMILIAN. Who is this man?

RUPF. Otto Rupf. President and Chairman of the Board of Rupf Pants and Vest.

AEMILIAN. What do you want?

RUPF. A straight answer to my proposition. I can still save the Empire ... though it's going to be a bit more expensive than I thought.

AEMILIAN. Save the Empire?

RUPF. But I'll keep my end of the bargain. Rupf's word is his bond. Now where's that Emperor? I'm a busy man. Time is money.

AEMILIAN. Is this man a lunatic?

TULLIUS. Certainly not! Ottaker will go back to Germany for ten million. This gentleman is willing to give us the ten million.

AEMILIAN. On condition?

TULLIUS. That the Princess Rea becomes Mrs. Otto Rupf.

AEMILIAN. Send for her.

TULLIUS. But I'm not at all sure ...

AEMILIAN. And assemble the court. Assemble the court! That's an order, Tullius.

(*He touches his dagger.*)

Quick!

(TULLIUS *goes.*)

You will have your answer immediately, O maker of pants!

TULLIUS (*off-stage*). Assemble the court! Court assemble! Assemble. Assemble. Assemble the court!

(TITUS *reappears right, staggering.*)

TITUS. I'm ready to drop. A hundred, hundred hours, no sleep. Tired. Tired.

(*He sits on a stool.* JULIA *and* REA *enter from the upstage door.*)

JULIA. Aemilian. We thought you were dead!

AEMILIAN (*kneels*). I am dead.

JULIA. Yes, of course.

(*She moves toward him.*)

We're all so happy to have you back. But nine years is a long time and things are not what they were, and ... ah, there's dear Mr. Rupf.

(*She crosses to* RUPF; *she beams.*)

RUPF. Empress, you're bankrupt.

JULIA (*frowns*). Oh, dear.

RUPF. But I still plan to go ahead with the merger.

JULIA (*smiles*). Good!

RUPF. A deal's a deal.

JULIA. Rea, come and meet Mr. Rupf.

(REA *steps down left to him.*)

RUPF. Nice to meet you, young lady. Real pleasure. *Real* pleasure.

(*He takes her hand and kisses it.*)

JULIA. He's such a gentleman. Isn't he, Rea? Isn't he good. And kind?

(*She turns to* AEMILIAN.)

Aemilian, you must understand our position. You must be reasonable. I know it's a shock to you, Rea falling in love with Mr. Rupf ...

REA. Mother!

AEMILIAN (*to* REA). Come here.

JULIA. Careful!

AEMILIAN (*to* REA). Do you love me?

REA. Do I love death? If death is Aemilian, I love death.

(RUPF *comes toward them.*)

RUPF. What's this?

JULIA. Rea! (*Pleading.*) Aemilian, help us.

AEMILIAN. Love with all your soul?

REA. With all my soul, I love you, death.

AEMILIAN. Would you do anything I asked you to do?

REA. Name it. I will do it.

AEMILIAN. Then marry this fat fool and bear him children as fat and foolish as he!

TULLIUS. Oh, God.

JULIA (*to* RUPF, *quickly*). He didn't really mean that, of course, about your weight and intelligence. They learn to talk that way in the army.

RUPF. Oh, I know the sort. Just envy, that's all. Quite used to it. When you close a big deal like this you learn to take the rough with the smooth.

AEMILIAN (*to* REA). Now give the clown your hand. (*To* RUPF.) Otto Rupf, the daughter of all the Caesars will be your wife.

RUPF. Princess, you have to believe me when I say how moved I am. Really moved. These tears are real tears of happiness. Rupf Incorporated ...

(*Shakes hands with* METELLUS, TULLIUS *and* ZENO.)

... now stands organically at the pinnacle of the business world. Rupf Incorporated has done it again. The competition will be fit to be tied!

METELLUS. The Empire is saved without a battle!

TULLIUS. We must save the archives! (*Calls off stage right.*) Stop the burning!

ZENO. Now in a hearty voice, three hosannas, and one jubilation!

CROWD. Hosanna! Hosanna! Hosanna! Jubilation!

(ACHILLES *calls from stage right.*)

ACHILLES. Make way for the Divine Caesar!

(ROMULUS, ACHILLES *and* PYRAMUS *appear. All drop to their knees except* JULIA *and* AEMILIAN.)

ALL TOGETHER. Hail Caesar! Hail! Hail!

ROMULUS. Hail. I must say, everyone seems to be in a good mood. Why?

AEMILIAN. Hail, Caesar! Emperor of three meals a day! Lord of the chickens! All hail, to the one we soldiers call Romulus the Little!

(*There is a gasp of horror.*)

ROMULUS. When people become rude to one's face it is a sign that one's day is just about over.

PYRAMUS. Shall we execute him, Divine Caesar?

(ROMULUS *examines* AEMILIAN *carefully.*)

ROMULUS. Aemilian. I might have known.

AEMILIAN. You are the only one to have recognized me. Not even your daughter knew me.

ROMULUS. But never doubt her love. It's just that the vision of age is sometimes more acute than that of youth. You're thin. You have been hungry.

AEMILIAN. While I starved, you ate well.

ROMULUS. True. Welcome, Aemilian.

(*He tries to take* AEMILIAN'*s hand.* AEMILIAN *pulls back.*)

AEMILIAN. I'm sorry, Divine Caesar. My manners are rude. I've been a prisoner too long. I've forgotten court etiquette.

ROMULUS. You cannot offend me. (*He takes the wounded arm.*) I see by your hand that you were tortured.

AEMILIAN. I was tortured while you raised chickens.

ROMULUS. Yet which of us, do you think, was the more usefully employed?

AEMILIAN. When I escaped in the north, I walked from one end of Italy to the other. I saw it all.

ROMULUS. Tell me about my Empire, Aemilian. I've never seen it, you know. I never leave Tivoli.

AEMILIAN. I saw the ruin of a world.

ROMULUS. And my subjects?

AEMILIAN. Our people are looted and raped by Gothic soldiers. They are cheated by profiteers. And there is no justice.

ROMULUS (*thoughtfully*). No justice ... Yes, I have heard the same reports.

AEMILIAN. But how can you know what you have never seen?

ROMULUS. I have ... imagination. Now come inside. My daughter has waited long enough.

AEMILIAN. I am unworthy to be received by her.

ROMULUS. You are not unworthy.

AEMILIAN. But I am! Humiliated! Treated like an animal by the Goths! Forced to crawl naked beneath a bloody yoke!

REA. Aemilian ...

(REA *tries to embrace* AEMILIAN. *He pushes her from him.*)

AEMILIAN. Rea, go to our savior.

(REA *obediently crosses to* RUPF.)

ROMULUS. Savior? What are you talking about? Rea, come here. (*To* RUPF.) I shall attend to you presently, Mr. Rupf.

AEMILIAN. Not presently. *Now*. Rupf will save us all. Through our shame, Rome will survive. Give him your blessing, Caesar. He is not only your savior. He is about to become your son-in-law.

JULIA. Heaven be praised! Dear Mr. Rupf, I welcome you into the family.

RUPF (*moved*). May I call you ... Mother?

JULIA (*pluckily*). Of course.

RUPF. Me, Otto Rupf, son-in-law to the Emperor. A dream come true.

JULIA (*to* REA). Child, you have saved Rome! Be lieve me, your sacrifice will be remembered ...

RUPF (*taken aback*). Sacrifice? Now really, Mother, I'm not exactly what you'd call the *worst* husband in the world. By a long shot. After all, I'm rich. Good-looking, in an organic sort of way, everyone says so ...

ROMULUS (*coldly*). Shut up, fool. We do not sanction this marriage. It will not take place.

(*Consternation.*)

RUPF (*stricken*). But ... Dad!

(ROMULUS *shuts his eyes in mock horror.*)

REA (*to* ROMULUS). Father, I *must* marry him. It's what Aemilian wants.

JULIA. You cannot stop her.

ROMULUS. I can stop her. And I will. I am still Emperor, for a few more hours anyway. (*To* REA.) I am also your father. You will do as I tell you. Now go inside.

REA. You see, Aemilian? He will not let us have your comic ending.

(REA *starts to go.*)

JULIA (*to* ROMULUS). You ... idiot!

AEMILIAN. Do you realize that this is the end of all of us?

ROMULUS. No. The beginning. (*He pulls* REA *to him.*) Of your life with Rea. You love her. She loves you ...

AEMILIAN (*scornfully*). "Love!" Now? Listen, little Emperor, I also bring you news: Rome, the city of Rome has fallen.

(*The sky darkens. Far-off cries begin to sound, mournful and strange.*)

ROMULUS (*softly*). At last.

AEMILIAN. The Goths have taken the city. They will be here tomorrow. Ottaker will be here tomorrow. The Butcher will be here in your palace tomorrow! He will have your head! He has said he will have your head on a pike tomorrow!

(*Horror from the assemblage. Repetition: "The monster! the butcher! the killer!"*)

AEMILIAN. Only Rea can save us. There is still time.

ROMULUS (*finality*). There is no time left for Rome. But there is time for you. There is time for Rea. There is time for life. Take it.

AEMILIAN. I cannot.

ROMULUS. You are ... perverse, Aemilian. You have been dishonored, or so you think.

AEMILIAN. I have been dishonored. I know.

ROMULUS. Your body ... your flesh, abused by enemies.

AEMILIAN. Abused. Tortured. Broken.

ROMULUS. Humiliated?

AEMILIAN. Humiliated.

ROMULUS. And now you want your revenge?

AEMILIAN. Yes!

ROMULUS. But revenge not on the enemy. Not on the Goths. You want your revenge on Rea.

REA. Father!

ROMULUS. Yes, my dear. He wants you hurt, abused, humiliated, as he was. The only way he can love you now is to see you defiled the way he was defiled. He would give you to this creature in order that he might revel at the thought of your shame. Lust at the thought of you in that fat embrace ...

AEMILIAN (*near breaking*). Stop!

REA. Aemilian, is it true what he says?

AEMILIAN. I don't matter. You don't matter. (*To* ROMULUS.) But Rome does.

ROMULUS. No. Rome does not matter now. It is too late to patch together this falling time. The Emperor knows what he is doing when he throws his Empire into the flames, when he lets fall what is already broken and buries what is already dead. This marriage will not take place.

JULIA. Romulus!

ROMULUS (*coldly*). That is my will.

(*A long sigh from the assemblage.* ROMULUS *turns to* PYRAMUS *and* ACHILLES; *lightly.*)

And now I think we've had enough chatter for one day. So back to work! Pyramus, the chicken feed!

(PYRAMUS *hands* ROMULUS *the basket. Accompanied by* PYRAMUS *and* ACHILLES, ROMULUS *goes off stage right, scattering grain.*)

Here Augustus, Tiberius, Claudius ... Here Trajan, Hadrian, Pertinax ... Here chicky-chick-chick.

(*A sound of firing off-stage; the sky is red.*)

SCENE 2

Midnight.

There is a moon. In the center of the audience chamber a bed has been placed. ROMULUS *appears in the garden from stage right. He comes down stage center, he looks about.*

ROMULUS (*thoughtfully*). The last night. The last look at the last moon. Then tomorrow and the last sun. Then ... what?

(*Pauses, touches a leaf, a flower.*)

Green – red – will there be color? Or just blackness.

(*Holds out hand.*)

Am I afraid? The hand is steady.

(*Behind him* AEMILIAN *in a black cloak appears at stage left. He pauses, sword drawn.*)

Even so ... what is next?

(PYRAMUS *and* ACHILLES *enter with lamp. The room is illuminated.* ROMULUS *turns.*)

What's that bed doing here?

ACHILLES. It is the best we could find, Divine Caesar.

PYRAMUS. The Empress ...

ACHILLES. May she live a thousand years ...

PYRAMUS. Has sent your bedroom furniture on to Sicily ...

ACHILLES. General Delivery ...

ROMULUS. Why did she send *my* bed?

(AEMILIAN *slips off-stage.*)

ACHILLES. Apparently it belonged to her father.

ROMULUS. How sentimental of her! Well, it's a warm night. This is quite pleasant.

PYRAMUS. The Empress has just requested audience.

ROMULUS. Audience not granted. No visitors tonight. Except my daughter.

(*Almost as an afterthought,* ROMULUS *removes wreath and gives it to* PYRAMUS.)

Oh, my poor old laurel wreath. I must have had it on in the bath. Hang it on that peg over there.

(PYRAMUS *does so.*)

How many leaves are left?

PYRAMUS. Only two, Divine Caesar.

ROMULUS. Not only has it been a sad day ... it has been an expensive one.

(*Sighs; then a deep breath.*)

Fresh air at last! The smoke's all gone. I must say, disastrous though the day has been, at least we got the archives burnt. Probably the greatest contribution I could have made to history.

PYRAMUS. Historians will forever lament Divine Caesar's decision.

ROMULUS. Nonsense. If there is anything an historian hates, it is a fact. I have now set their imaginations free. Henceforth, the story of Rome will be a department of creative writing.

(*He sits on divan.*)

Bring me my Catullus. I shall read a few lines.

(*Looks at the two.*)

Or has my wife packed the library because the library belonged to her father?

PYRAMUS. She has done exactly that, Divine Caesar.

ROMULUS. Then pour me some wine. At least the wine did not belong to her father ... unfortunately. We've drunk all those splendid years.

(PYRAMUS *pours some wine. The door opens.* JULIA *stands silhouetted.* ACHILLES, *who is nearest to her, crosses to her.*)

JULIA (*furiously*). Out of my way! Romulus, you will see me!
ROMULUS. Not only will I see you, I *do* see you.
JULIA. You cannot keep me out! Pyramus, Achilles, withdraw.
ROMULUS. Stay.
JULIA. I am *hereditary* Empress. Achilles ... Pyramus, obey!
(*They go.*)
ROMULUS. Don't you think you're pressing your luck a bit, Julia? I am still capable of an act of domestic violence. In the great tradition of my predecessors.
JULIA. Kill me! I couldn't care less, only let Mr. Rupf marry Rea and save Rome.
ROMULUS. No. Such a marriage would be unthinkable. Did you hear him? He called me "Dad." It was chilling.
JULIA. Then you must come with us to Sicily. Tonight.
ROMULUS. The Emperor does not flee. Did Tullius find you a proper boat?
JULIA. No. A raft.
ROMULUS. A raft? Oh, you'd better not go. You know you're a bad sailor. You'll be horribly seasick. Also, rafts are dangerous.
JULIA. Far more dangerous to stay here. With you. I shall reassemble the government in Sicily. We shall fight on against the enemy. We shall save the world, no matter what the cost!
ROMULUS. What a sense of theatre you have. Come off it, Julia. You're going to fight for yourself ... not the world.
JULIA. Myself? I have no self. I am Rome.
ROMULUS. Are you really? I was never quite certain.
JULIA. If you *don't* come with us, the Goths will kill you.
ROMULUS. It would certainly be out of character if they did not.
JULIA. I see. (*A new track.*) Romulus, we have been married twenty years. We were in love.
ROMULUS. What an extraordinary thing to mention! I thought your particular field was politics. Certainly not marital relations. Julia, you shock me! I've never heard you make such a ... *personal* remark to anyone.

JULIA. I have been impersonal because that is what you wanted me to be. Nevertheless, we were in love once.

ROMULUS. You are stark staring mad.

JULIA. Do you mean to say that you married me *only* to become Emperor?

ROMULUS. No, that is not what I meant to say. But now that *you* have brought the subject up: yes, that is why I married you.

JULIA. You dare tell me this to my face?

ROMULUS. I would certainly never say it behind your back. In my way, I try to be a gentleman. But I believe I do not exaggerate when I say that our marriage has been as close to hell on earth as any marriage I have ever heard of.

JULIA. And for that hell on earth, I hate you.

ROMULUS. And I like you for that. Hate is a pure emotion. But do give me credit for never once having pretended to love you. We were both very practical people. I married you to become Emperor. You married me to become Empress. There is something very clean about that. The motive in each case was intelligent self-interest.

JULIA. True. We needed each other then, and we need each other now. Romulus, you must come with me to Sicily. We belong together, whether we like it or not. It is our destiny.

ROMULUS. I think not. I made you Empress and that's quite enough destiny for you. Your schemes paid off.

JULIA. And what about your schemes? Have they paid off?

ROMULUS (*nods*). They are about to. (*Thoughtfully.*) Today you said that you had never understood me. I was struck by that. And now that we are both in this curious mood of candor, let me say that I have never understood you. I have never understood people who were ambitious for *personal* power.

JULIA. Never understood it? You? My dear Romulus, you have just confessed that you married me to make yourself master of Rome. If that was not personal ambition, what was it?

ROMULUS. Necessity. What was an end for you was a means for me. I became Emperor for a certain purpose, through political cunning.

JULIA (*scornfully*). Political cunning! During the whole of your reign you have done nothing but eat and sleep and raise your damned chickens. Not once have you appeared in the city of Rome. You have sat here in this house, absolutely still, as the state collapsed about us. Your only gift is your wit which manages to crush opposition. Political cunning! Nero and Caligula in their madness were statesmen of vision compared to you! You do nothing! You are nothing!

ROMULUS (*coolly*). But don't you see, Julia? *That* is my political cunning: that was my plan: to do nothing. Nothing at all.

JULIA. You didn't have to become an Emperor to do nothing.

ROMULUS. Of course I did. Otherwise my idleness had no meaning. To be idle as a private citizen would have been perfectly useless, and rather immoral.

JULIA. While to be idle as an Emperor merely endangers the state?

ROMULUS (*softly*). Exactly.

(JULIA *is startled.*)

JULIA. And what does that mean?

ROMULUS. That means you have finally discovered the secret of my idleness.

JULIA (*disbelieving*). You *wanted* to endanger the state?

ROMULUS (*nods*). I wanted to endanger the state.

JULIA. But why? The state is necessary.

ROMULUS. I don't deny the necessity of the state in general. I just deny the necessity of *this* state. Our state. Rome.

JULIA. If you believed that, then why did you, of all people, want to become Emperor?

ROMULUS. Because only the Emperor can ... liquidate the Empire.

JULIA. And that is why you married me.

ROMULUS. That is why I married you.

JULIA. From the beginning, you wanted Rome destroyed?

ROMULUS. From the beginning.

JULIA. You have consciously and knowingly sabotaged all efforts to save us.

ROMULUS. Consciously and knowingly.

JULIA. You have played the cynic, the clown, the buffoon, simply to trick us.

ROMULUS (*smiles*). I wouldn't have put it quite that way, but you seem to have got the general point. (*Rises.*) At last we understand each other, Julia. The masks are down.

JULIA. I was right. You are mad.

(JULIA *turns to go.*)

ROMULUS (*rises*). Good-bye, Julia. Have a nice trip. Sicily should be great fun this time of year. Especially the beach. But don't get too much sun all at once. You know how easily you burn.

(JULIA *pauses at the door.*)

JULIA. What you have done you will regret. You cannot play fate. You are not God. As you have judged us, so shall you be judged. And I pray that when you are you will be shown no mercy.

(JULIA *goes.* ROMULUS *sits for a moment thoughtfully. Then claps his hands.* PYRAMUS *enters.*)

ROMULUS. Pyramus, more wine.

PYRAMUS. Yes, Divine Caesar.

(PYRAMUS *pours wine. His hand shakes.*)

ROMULUS. My dear fellow, you're shaking like a leaf. What's wrong?

PYRAMUS. Divine Caesar does not like us to mention the military situation to him.

ROMULUS. No. I don't like it at all. I discuss military affairs only with my barber. He is the one person I know who seems to understand such things.

PYRAMUS. Divine Caesar, your bodyguard has deserted.

ROMULUS (*lightly*). Stout hearts and true! Grant them the title: "The Heroes of Tivoli."

(PYRAMUS *gives* ROMULUS *the goblet.*)

PYRAMUS. They fled because the Goths are just a few miles from Tivoli.

(PYRAMUS *spills some wine on* ROMULUS.)

ROMULUS. That is no reason for spilling good wine, and staining my dressing gown.

PYRAMUS. A thousand apologies, Divine Caesar.

ROMULUS. I'm sorry. Go to bed.

(*As* PYRAMUS *goes,* ACHILLES *enters. He stands at the door.*)

ACHILLES. The Princess Rea begs audience of Caesar.

(REA *appears just behind him.*)

ROMULUS. Oh, good. Come in, my dear.

REA. Mother wants me to go to Sicily tonight. With her. But I don't want to go. I don't want to leave you.

ROMULUS. Darling, we must all do things we don't want to do. You must go where you will be safe.

REA. No. We must all stay here. Aemilian says we can still save the state.

ROMULUS. How curious that tonight everyone should want to talk politics. Lunch is the time for politics. Not after supper.

REA. What else should I talk about?

ROMULUS. There are special things a girl talks to her father about at night. Such as: What is closest to her heart.

REA. Rome is closest to my heart.

ROMULUS. You no longer love Aemilian?

REA. Oh, yes.

ROMULUS. But not as much as you did?

REA. More! I love him more than life.

ROMULUS. Then talk to me about Aemilian.

REA. Aemilian says I must marry Otto Rupf.

ROMULUS. My dear, Otto Rupf has a certain appeal. I don't doubt it. I particularly like his money. But you don't love him and even if you did, he makes me uneasy.

REA. He will save Rome.

ROMULUS. But that's exactly what makes me uneasy. Any pants manufacturer who wants to save the Roman Empire must be a bit mad. Or an incurable romantic. Of course, businessmen *tend* to be romantic. Sentimental. Impractical. Business is often the last refuge of the artist. Nevertheless ...

REA. Father, there's no one else *can* save us!

ROMULUS. True. But a country which can be saved only by money is a lost country anyway. After all, what *is* the choice, really? On the one hand: catastrophic capitalism, and on the other a capital catastrophe. Where's Pyramus? I must get him to write that down.

REA. But no matter what, my country comes first.

ROMULUS. Dear girl, you've been reading too much tragedy.

REA. I couldn't live without my patriotism.

ROMULUS. Could you live without your young man? Yes. Perhaps. It is harder to keep faith with a human being than with a country. My darling, forget your play acting, marry Aemilian and make yourself ... and your father ... happy.

REA. Aemilian has rejected me.

ROMULUS. I don't believe it.

REA. He knows what I must do. That's why he doesn't love me any more. He loves Rome.

ROMULUS. Well, luckily for you, Rome is about to perish. Then he will have nothing left to love but you. You'll get him back. I promise.

REA. I'm so afraid.

ROMULUS. You must learn to conquer your fear. That is the one art we can master in this twilight time. To look at things as they are, without fear. To do the right thing no matter how hard, without fear. I've spent my life practicing *not* to be afraid. You practice, too. Now go to Aemilian ... You know, Rea, you are all that I ever allowed myself to care for.

(REA *clings to him.*)

And I care for you in spite of myself because I've known all along what was to come. I knew how it would end and I wanted to regret nothing.

REA. How will it end?

ROMULUS. As it ought. Now. No more tears. Remember what I've told you. And look at me for the last time.

REA. No! Escape with us! Father ... please!

ROMULUS. I cannot. Why, if I were to survive, my life would be a complete failure. (*More lightly.*) It would lack ... symmetry.

REA. And you think *I* play act.

ROMULUS (*smiles*). A good point. Yes, I play act, too. We're very much alike, aren't we? (*Firmly.*) But my performance is necessary. Now go, be brave ...

REA. Please, come with us ...

ROMULUS. Forget Rome. Marry Aemilian. Be happy. Quickly now, no more speeches. No tears. Go!

(REA *goes.* AEMILIAN *appears upstage, behind* ROMULUS, *who starts to drink; as he does, he sees* AEMILIAN *reflected in the goblet.* PYRAMUS *enters.* AEMILIAN *steps behind a column.*)

PYRAMUS. Is the Divine Caesar ready to retire?

ROMULUS. No, not yet. Another goblet.

PYRAMUS. Another ... ?

ROMULUS. Yes. There is someone else I must talk to.

(PYRAMUS *fills the goblet.*)

Now, off to bed with you.

(PYRAMUS *bows and withdraws.*)

All right, Aemilian. (*Without turning.*) We're alone at last.

(AEMILIAN *emerges from the shadows.*)

AEMILIAN. How did you know I was here?

ROMULUS. I saw you reflected in the goblet. (*Serenely.*) Pyramus keeps them beautifully polished, don't you think? Have some wine. It's poured. Do sit down.

AEMILIAN. I stand.

ROMULUS. As you please. Isn't this rather late for a visit? It's midnight.

AEMILIAN. Some visits are made only at midnight.

ROMULUS. How ominous you make it sound! Nevertheless, I am ready for you ... with a delicious wine. Let us drink to each other's health.

AEMILIAN. So be it.

ROMULUS. And to your return from slavery.

AEMILIAN. And to what I must do this night.

ROMULUS. To that. By all means, to *that!*

(*They drink.*)

AEMILIAN. And now a toast to justice, Divine Caesar!

ROMULUS (*more seriously*). Oh? I hope you realize that justice on earth is relative. And sometimes terrible.

AEMILIAN. As terrible as my scars?

ROMULUS. To justice.

(*They drink.*)

I suppose you will leave with Rea tonight?

AEMILIAN. I hope we shall not be forced to leave.

ROMULUS. You know she loves you. Take good care of her when I am gone.

AEMILIAN. When you are gone, she will be taken good care of.

(AEMILIAN *draws his sword.* ROMULUS *steps back to the bed. There is a scream.* TULLIUS *appears from under the bed, wringing his hand.*)

ROMULUS. Good heavens, what was that?

TULLIUS (*reproachfully*). You stepped on my fingers, Divine Caesar!

ROMULUS. Tullius! I *am* sorry. Really terribly sorry. But how was I to know you were *under* my bed?

TULLIUS (*gabbling*). I just happened to get *under* the bed to work on my new tax program, completely voluntary, of course. I have the memorandum right here.

(TULLIUS *gets to his feet during this. He wears a black cloak.*)

ROMULUS. Look! Your hand is bleeding.

TULLIUS. Oh dear! I must've scratched myself on the dagger ... I mean on the pen I was writing with.

ROMULUS. Such a sharp pen, for such a sharp and astute political mind.

AEMILIAN (*ominously*). Does the Divine Caesar wish to call the palace guard?

ROMULUS. How can I? They've fled. As you well know. But we must get something to bandage poor Tullius's hand.

(*He crosses to the cupboard left. As he opens it,* ZENO, *cloaked in black, falls into the room.*)

ROMULUS. Zeno! I didn't know you liked to sleep in closets. I'm sorry I waked you. Go back to bed.

ZENO (*gabbling*). No, no. That's all right. I'm wide awake now. You know it's got to be a habit with me, closets. I've had to put up with so many hardships since I left home that I feel, well, more comfy in a closet.

ROMULUS. I couldn't be sorrier, disturbing you like this.

ZENO (*to* ROMULUS). Don't let me interrupt you.

ROMULUS (*amused*). That's perfectly all right. We're just burning the midnight oil.

(ROMULUS *gives* TULLIUS *the cloth.*)

Here, Tullius, bandage yourself. I can't bear the sight of blood. (*Turns.*) And now if there is anyone else hidden in my bedroom, will he – or they – please come forth.

(METELLUS *appears from right, wearing a black cloak.*)

METELLUS. Just happened to be in the neighborhood and thought I might drop in and chew the fat with you about this total mobilization thing.

(*From the left the* CHEF *appears; he wears a black cloak, white hat. For the first time* ROMULUS *is shaken.*)

ROMULUS. *Et tu,* Chef?

(*The* CHEF *joins the semicircle which now menaces the Emperor who is downstage.*)

All of you wear black, I see. I suppose that is the proper shade for conspiracy.

AEMILIAN (*coldly*). Black is the color of midnight, and of justice.

ROMULUS. I'm sorry to have put you all to such great inconvenience. Poor creatures, you've spent half the night under beds and in closets, in the most complicated positions! And as for those extraordinary costumes – why even you, Tullius, manage to look sinister. I'm very proud of you.

TULLIUS. We want to talk to you.

ROMULUS. I thought you had something like that in mind. (*Sits at the table.*) The Emperor is ready to hear his loyal subjects.

TULLIUS. We demand the return of the provinces.

METELLUS. The return of the legions.

CHEF. The return of good living.

ZENO. The return of classical culture.

AEMILIAN. The return of the Empire.

ROMULUS. The Emperor is accountable to no man.

AEMILIAN. But *this* Emperor owes Rome an accounting.

ZENO. Yes, Romulus. You must vindicate yourself before history. You must explain why you have allowed barbarism to engulf us.

TULLIUS. You must explain why you have ignored the business of the state.

METELLUS. You must explain why you have allowed our military power to collapse.

ROMULUS (*reasonably*). But there is nothing to explain. If I had conquered the world with your help you might be entitled to talk as you do. But I have lost a world which you did not win.

ZENO. But you let go what was left.

TULLIUS. You had no faith in us.

AEMILIAN. You refuse to believe that we are great.

ROMULUS. We were great. But that was before any of *us* was born. To be wise is to be able to recognize a fact. The fact is that Rome is lost. And now that that world is finally lost, I am free and you are no concern of mine, any of you. You are just ... moths, dancing around the light I give, shadows which will vanish when I no longer shine.

AEMILIAN (*gestures*). The light.

(*Conspirators put out the lights. The only illumination is from a candle on the table beside* ROMULUS, *and the moonlight.*)

ROMULUS For only one of you have I ... compassion. Aemilian.

(AEMILIAN *approaches.*)

AEMILIAN. Remember, Romulus, *you* are on trial.

ROMULUS. No. Not I. You. Your midnight court has been convened but *I* sit in judgment. Yet to you, Aemilian, I will speak as one man to another, as father to son.

AEMILIAN. It is too late in the night to win me, Romulus.

ROMULUS. Win? There is nothing to win. You are quite lost. All of you. But I do care for you, Aemilian, even as I pass sentence. I understand you. I pity you. For you are that perennial phenomenon, the human being who is sacrificed to the state. Your body twisted, your mind twisted ... Out of pity I will answer only you.

AEMILIAN. Then answer.

ROMULUS. Ask the question.

AEMILIAN. What have you done to prevent Rome from being humiliated as I was humiliated?

ROMULUS. Nothing.

AEMILIAN. Then I accuse you of having betrayed Rome.

(*A murmur from the others.*)

ROMULUS. No! *I* did not betray Rome. Rome betrayed herself. Long ago. Rome knew truth, but chose power. Rome knew humaneness, but chose tyranny. Rome debased herself, as well as those she governed ... that is a double curse. You stand, Aemilian, before the throne of the Roman Emperors. That throne is not visible to you, is it? To any of you. But it is most visible to its occupant, to me, its *last* occupant. This throne is set upon a mountain of empty grinning skulls, streams of blood gush upon the steps to this high place where Caesar sits, where *I* sit, presiding over those cataracts of blood which are the source of power. And now you demand an answer from this high place where I sit upon the bodies of my sons and the hecatombs of my enemies. (*Rises.*) Very well, you shall have your answer. Rome is old and weak and staggering, but her debt is not yet paid, nor her crimes forgotten. But the hour of judgment is near. The old tree is dying. The ax is ready. The Goths have come. We who have bled others must now ourselves be bled. You have asked for justice. I shall give it! I sentence Rome to death!

AEMILIAN. Hail, Rome!

(*All draw their daggers. They close in on* ROMULUS.)

EACH CONSPIRATOR. Kill him! Kill him! Kill him! Kill him!

(AEMILIAN *puts his dagger to* ROMULUS' *throat.*)

AEMILIAN. Here is justice, Caesar. The knife!

(*From off-stage, pandemonium.*)

VOICES. The Goths! Run! Help! Save us! The Goths!

(PYRAMUS *and* ACHILLES *rush into the room. The conspirators panic. In a moment all have escaped, each in a different direction.* ROMULUS *sinks onto the bench.*)

ACHILLES. Is the Divine Caesar hurt?

ROMULUS (*softly*). No.

PYRAMUS. Traitors! Traitors!

ROMULUS. No, not traitors. It is too late even for treason. There are only victims now. Where are the Goths exactly?

(ROMULUS *crosses upstage to the table.*)

PYRAMUS. In Tivoli, in the town, Divine Caesar.

ROMULUS. Then why so much commotion? They won't get to the palace until morning.

(*He is about to pour himself wine, when a robed, sleeping figure rolls out from under the bed.*)

ROMULUS. Oh, no, not another one! Who is it!

(ACHILLES *peers at the sleeping figure.*)

ACHILLES. It is the young Prefect, Titus.

ROMULUS (*smiles*). Asleep at last.

PYRAMUS. Shall we remove him?

ROMULUS. No. Let him alone. Put a blanket over him.

(PYRAMUS *puts a blanket over* TITUS. *Then, with* ACHILLES, *he is about to withdraw.* ROMULUS *stops him.*)

ROMULUS. Oh, Pyramus ...

PYRAMUS. Yes, Divine Caesar?

ROMULUS. When Ottaker the Butcher arrives show him in directly. With style.

(*They go. Thoughtfully,* ROMULUS *drinks ... as though he had proposed a toast.*)

ACT THREE

It is the morning of March 16, 476 A.D. *The busts are gone from their niches.* ACHILLES *and* PYRAMUS *are tidying up. They place a number of wilted laurel wreaths about the room.*

ACHILLES. A lovely morning!

PYRAMUS. It is amazing that the sun dares to rise on a day of such despair.

ACHILLES. Nature was always unreliable.

PYRAMUS. Only think, for sixty years, under eleven Emperors ...

ACHILLES. We have served Rome.

PYRAMUS. I simply cannot believe that the whole world should end in our lifetime.

(*Shakes wreath.*)

What a lot of dust!

ACHILLES. Fortunately, no one can accuse us of not doing our part. When we go, they will say: That is the end of antiquity.

PYRAMUS. And the beginning of ... what is the word, Achilles?

ACHILLES. "Modern." The beginning of the modern.

PYRAMUS. I predict that this "modern" era will be known as the dark ages.

ACHILLES. No doubt of it. (*Starts.*) I hear him. Will you tell him, or shall I?

PYRAMUS. I cannot give him such tragic news.

(ROMULUS *enters from upstage. He is in full regalia.*)

ACHILLES AND PYRAMUS. Hail, Caesar!

ROMULUS. Hail! I'm late. There was an enormous crowd at the audience this morning. Everyone wants a visa or a passport ... I can't think where they expect to go. I see you've tidied up nicely. Quite festive! I hope our friend the Gothic Butcher appreciates our efforts. I'm hungry. Where's my breakfast?

PYRAMUS. In a moment, Divine Caesar, your egg will be ready.

ROMULUS (*to* ACHILLES). Do I look haggard?

ACHILLES. The Divine Caesar never looked more glorious!

(ROMULUS *picks up the watering can and crosses to the downstage plants.*)

ROMULUS. I don't think I slept more than an hour last night. That young Prefect not only snores, he grinds his teeth. What did you do with him?

PYRAMUS. We placed him in the garden.

ACHILLES. He is still asleep.

PYRAMUS. Does the Divine Caesar know that the Goths have surrounded the palace?

ROMULUS. Yes. Do you know I believe I did more ruling last night than I have in all the twenty years of my reign.

(*He has finished watering the first plant. He notices the table* ACHILLES *has set for him.*)

What ugly plates! All chipped and cracked. Where is the Imperial service?

ACHILLES. The Empress took it with her last night.

ROMULUS. Ah, yes. It was her father's. Well, perhaps broken pieces are more fitting for a last meal.

(*Crosses to second plant.*)

There was a storm early this morning, wasn't there?

PYRAMUS (*nods*). At about dawn.

ROMULUS. Poor Julia. She was never a good sailor. She must have suffered. (*Suddenly.*) Why is it so quiet? I have the odd feeling we're alone. Absolutely alone here. Just the three of us.

PYRAMUS. We are alone, Divine Caesar.

ACHILLES. We are all that's left.

ROMULUS. But where is Tullius? Where's Metellus? Where's my cook?

PYRAMUS. They left with the Empress for Sicily.

ROMULUS. Oh? The government-in-exile, of course. And my daughter, Rea?

(ACHILLES *and* PYRAMUS *exchange an uneasy glance.*)

ACHILLES. She is gone, too.

ROMULUS. With the Empress?

PYRAMUS. With the Empress.

ROMULUS. And Aemilian.

PYRAMUS. He is with the Princess.

(ROMULUS *puts down watering can; he goes to the breakfast table.*)

ROMULUS. Good. Good. At least one thing has worked out well for us. They will marry. They will be happy.

(ROMULUS, *standing, drinks from a goblet.*)

PYRAMUS. No, Divine Caesar. They will not marry. They will not be happy.

ACHILLES. They were all drowned.

(ROMULUS *puts down the goblet. He turns, stunned.*)

PYRAMUS. This morning.

ACHILLES. In the storm.

PYRAMUS. The raft was dashed to pieces.

ACHILLES. Near Ostia.

PYRAMUS. The Empress, the court, all are dead.

ACHILLES. A fisherman brought us the news while you were holding audience.

ROMULUS (*slowly*). My daughter Rea and Aemilian dead. (*He looks at them.*) I see no tear in your eyes.

ACHILLES. We are old.

ROMULUS. True. And you will die very soon yourselves, in the natural course.

PYRAMUS. Yes, Divine Caesar.

ROMULUS. And I shall die, too. Even sooner. Today, in fact. The Goths will kill me. So he who is about to die would be somewhat ... excessive ... to mourn the dead. Serve the morning meal, Pyramus.

(PYRAMUS *removes cover from plates.* ROMULUS *breaks into egg.*)

ROMULUS (*mechanically*). Naturally, Augustus laid nothing.

ACHILLES. Nothing, Divine Caesar.

ROMULUS. Tiberius?

PYRAMUS. None of the Julians laid anything.

ROMULUS. Then whose is this?

PYRAMUS. Marcus Aurelius, as usual.

ROMULUS (*nods*). Did no one else lay?

PYRAMUS. Only ... Ottaker.

ROMULUS. Really?

PYRAMUS. Four eggs today, Divine Caesar!

ROMULUS (*delighted*). Good Heavens, that chicken has achieved greatness! Bestow upon her the title ... no, never mind. We have given our last title. (*Swallows wine.*) I must say, you both look unusually solemn.

ACHILLES. Divine Caesar, Otto Rupf has offered us positions in his household at Rome.

PYRAMUS. At the vulgar sum of four thousand a year. With three afternoons off a week.

ACHILLES. With such leisure we would have time to write our memoirs.

PYRAMUS. "Backstairs with the Twelve Caesars."

ACHILLES. The serial rights in Britain alone would keep us comfortably in our sunset years.

ROMULUS. I must say, if destiny did not have other plans for me, I might apply for a job with Mr. Rupf, too. You are free, of course. (*They cough with embarrassment.*) Oh, I forgot.

(*He takes off laurel wreath, breaks off last two leaves, and gives one to each.*)

The last two leaves from my crown. The last financial deal of my reign. They are yours. (*Sighs.*) I must say I have never been more at peace than I am now, when everything is over.

PYRAMUS. Does the Divine Caesar wish the Imperial Sword of Alexander?

ROMULUS. Didn't we pawn it?

ACHILLES. No pawnbroker would take it.

PYRAMUS. Too rusty. Shall I fetch it?

ROMULUS. No, dear Pyramus. It would be out of character. I prefer to go to my fate as I have lived, with a knife and fork, not a sword.

(*War cries in the garden.*)

What on earth is that?

ACHILLES. The Goths, Divine Caesar. They are here!

ROMULUS. At last. Well, I shall just have to receive them at breakfast ...

(PYRAMUS *and* ACHILLES, *terrified, edge toward the door.*)

PYRAMUS. Is everything satisfactory, Divine Caesar?

ROMULUS. Yes, you have done your work well. You both may go. Oh, when you write your memoirs, don't forget to mention that the last Emperor at his last meal ate heartily.

PYRAMUS AND ACHILLES. Hail, Caesar!

(*They withdraw, bowing.*)

ROMULUS. Hail.

(*He continues to eat thoughtfully, occasionally sipping wine; as he does, a* GOTH *enters, a middle-aged man dressed in trousers and military cloak. He is relaxed, but curious. He has the air of one visiting a museum. The only ominous note is the sword at his waist.* ROMULUS *watches him curiously, still eating. The* GOTH *ignores him. He examines the bust of Romulus, the Founder. Suddenly a large, muscular youth in battle gear enters. He sees* ROMULUS. *He draws a bayonet. He crosses to* ROMULUS *swiftly, grinning fiercely.* ROMULUS *remains very still.*)

YOUNG MAN. Die – Roman!

(*He is about to bring the sword down on* ROMULUS' *head when the* GOTH *turns to him.*)

GOTH. Stop that!

YOUNG MAN. Yes, dear Uncle.

GOTH (*indicates scabbard*). Bayonet!

YOUNG MAN. Yes, dear Uncle.

(YOUNG MAN *sheathes bayonet.*)

GOTH (*to* ROMULUS). Well?

ROMULUS. Well ... ? Oh, welcome to Tivoli. (*Doubtfully.*) You are Goths, aren't you?

GOTH. Can't you tell?

ROMULUS. As a matter of fact, no. According to Tacitus, all Goths have fierce blue eyes, long blond hair, and enormous muscles. Frankly, I'm disappointed. You look like a Byzantine botanist.

GOTH. We are both disappointed. Romans always run away from us. You are the first not to be frightened.

ROMULUS. I dare say there are misconceptions on both sides. Are you by any chance wearing trousers?

GOTH. What else?

ROMULUS. Such a remarkable garment! Where do you button it?

GOTH. In the front.

ROMULUS. How practical!

(*He drinks.*)

GOTH. What are you drinking?

ROMULUS. Asparagus wine.

GOTH. Oh?

(GOTH *takes a goblet.*)

ROMULUS. It's homemade.

(GOTH *drinks, shudders.*)

GOTH. Good God! We must show you Romans how to make beer. I congratulate you on your Venus. That one down by the pond, as you turn into the driveway.

ROMULUS. What about it?

GOTH. What about it? An original signed by Praxiteles. Worth a fortune.

ROMULUS. I have all the luck! I thought it was just a copy and now the art dealer's gone back to Utica. This is the last blow.

GOTH. I was told you had a fine collection of busts. Where are they?

ROMULUS. I sold them yesterday.

GOTH. Too bad. I wanted them for my palace.

ROMULUS. Then you ... you are Ottaker?

OTTAKER (*nods*). Prince of the Goths.

ROMULUS. Well ... well. We meet at last. How do you do? I am Romulus. You know? Emperor of Rome? (*Puts on wreath.*) SPQR?

OTTAKER. I knew who you were.

ROMULUS. I can't think how. That portrait they use on my coins was done years ago. (*Rises.*) Now I suppose you will need my head to decorate that pike of yours. I am ready.

OTTAKER. Good. Very good. You are brave. But first let me present my nephew. Bow, Theodoric.

THEODORIC (*bows*). Yes, dear Uncle.

OTTAKER. Deeper, nephew.

THEODORIC. Yes, dear Uncle.

OTTAKER. In fact, get down on your knees before the Emperor of Rome.

THEODORIC. Just as you say, dear Uncle.

(THEODORIC *is on his knees.*)

ROMULUS. Don't you think you are rather overdoing it?

OTTAKER. Now leave us, nephew.

THEODORIC. Yes, dear Uncle.

OTTAKER. Wait outside.

THEODORIC. Just as you say, dear Uncle.

(THEODORIC *goes.*)

ROMULUS. He will never forgive you for that.

OTTAKER (*abruptly*). What do you think of him?

ROMULUS (*taken aback*). What do *I* think of him? Well, a very polite young man. Yes, I was favorably impressed.

OTTAKER (*evenly*). Were you really? I'm not surprised. He's very polite. "Yes, dear Uncle. Just as you say, dear Uncle." He is a teetotaler. He sleeps on the floor. He practices every day with bayonet. At this very moment, he is outside there in the hall doing push-ups. He is perfect.

ROMULUS. In every way a classic hero.

OTTAKER (*nods*). You recognize the type. Naturally. You are classic, too.

(OTTAKER *draws his sword; he circles* ROMULUS, *sword pointed at his throat.*)

ROMULUS. I'm glad we're going to do this privately.

OTTAKER (*smiles pleasantly*). Yes. My people worship Theodoric. He is their ideal. He dreams of just one thing, the conquest of the world. You understand that, don't you?

ROMULUS. Yes. We used to have heroes like that. In fact, that's how we got started. Now, would you prefer to kill me here, or in the garden?

OTTAKER. Completely immaterial. Theodoric has inspired us all.

ROMULUS. I'm sure he has. I would prefer it here, but naturally if you have other plans, don't let me ...

OTTAKER. Don't rush me. You've heard of Gothic-ism?

ROMULUS. Oh, yes. We hate it, of course. But I've often wondered what it was.

OTTAKER. Theodoric invented Gothic-ism.

ROMULUS. But what is it?

OTTAKER. Make a guess.

ROMULUS. A rationale for the Gothic conquest of the world.

OTTAKER (*laughs*). Go to the head of the class.

ROMULUS. I was always good at examinations. Look, if we're going to chat, do you mind if I finish breakfast? It's getting a bit cold.

OTTAKER. Go right ahead.

(ROMULUS *sits at the breakfast table.*)

ROMULUS. Thank you. We used to have Roman-ism. But since we're so much older than you, we dropped the word. We now refer to the sacred heritage of classical culture. We conquered the world in order to give everyone a classical education. At least that's our story now. I'm not sure the world was grateful. But then, you should know. You were one of the races we educated.

(OTTAKER *sits at the table, too.*)

OTTAKER. Oh, yes. You were great educators. You taught us everything: greed, political murder, injustice.

ROMULUS. I am sorry. For what it is worth, I *am* sorry. Rome and I ask forgiveness for the past. In fact, I offer myself as final payment.

OTTAKER. Good. Reasonable. Acceptable. Yes. You are just. (*Nervously.*) What was that?

ROMULUS. You seem rather jumpy. I'm quite alone here. You're perfectly safe.

OTTAKER. I thought I heard him.

ROMULUS. Heard who?

OTTAKER. Theodoric.

(OTTAKER *goes upstage, peers through door.*)

ROMULUS. He makes you nervous, doesn't he?

(OTTAKER *prowls among the columns, sword ready.*)

OTTAKER (*angrily*). Nervous! You presume too much. Theodoric is a hero. Because of him I have conquered the world. Because of him my people have become a nation of heroes.

ROMULUS. A terrible fate – if I may say so – not only for the world, but also for the heroes.

OTTAKER. Yes. You are wise. Why do I doubt it? After all, I admired your book, "The Moral Principle in History."

ROMULUS. Really? Did you read it in the original version or the abridged?

OTTAKER. The original. I read all of it.

ROMULUS. How remarkable! No one here could ever get past the first chapter.

OTTAKER. But authors are seldom as good as their books. Now, one last question ...

ROMULUS (*smiles*). You do make it sound like an examination.

OTTAKER (*grimly*). That is exactly what it is. You are being examined, and graded.

ROMULUS. Graded? Like an egg?

(ROMULUS *automatically picks up an egg and taps it.*)

OTTAKER. Like a man. (*Interested.*) Do you know about eggs?

ROMULUS. Poultry is my passion.

(OTTAKER *takes the egg from him; he examines it, too; he is equally professional.*)

Yes. Do have an egg.

OTTAKER. From an Anatolian hen?

ROMULUS. That's right. Are you a chicken breeder?

OTTAKER. Yes.

ROMULUS. What a coincidence! So am I!

OTTAKER. You?

ROMULUS. All my life.

OTTAKER. Are those your chickens out there in the yard?

ROMULUS. Yes. Some are Anatolian. Some from a new breed in Gaul.

OTTAKER. Do they lay?

ROMULUS. Do you doubt it?

OTTAKER. Judging by this egg, no, not well ...

ROMULUS. You're right. And just between us chicken breeders, I'm a bit worried. They lay less and less. Only one hen is really up to the mark.

OTTAKER (*nods*). The gray one with the yellow spots?

ROMULUS. How did you know?

OTTAKER. Because I brought that particular breed into Italy. Wanted to see how it would do in a warm climate.

ROMULUS. Then, congratulations! It's done marvelously well.

OTTAKER. Thank you. My own breed.

ROMULUS (*impressed*). Yours? Then you must be a poultry man of the first rank.

OTTAKER (*modestly*). As Sovereign Father of my people I occasionally tend to useful matters. (*Recalls his grim task.*) Now: the last question. What do you think of me?

ROMULUS (*carefully*). I thought of you as the Gothic Butcher. The Scourge of God. Now I see that you are just a chicken breeder, like myself.

OTTAKER. The examination is complete.

ROMULUS. You will find me ready. You may proceed. I have had my breakfast. Would you prefer that I stood, or was seated?

OTTAKER. Immaterial.

ROMULUS. I shall sit.

(OTTAKER *draws his sword, as* ROMULUS *sits.*)

OTTAKER. My spies told me that Romulus was brave.

ROMULUS. Cowardly ...

OTTAKER. Wise.

ROMULUS. Foolish ...

OTTAKER. Just ...

ROMULUS. I have tried to be just.

OTTAKER. I didn't believe them.

ROMULUS. You were right not to. Your information agencies are as inaccurate as ours. Now, Ottaker, let us close the book of Rome.

(ROMULUS *shuts his eyes.*)

OTTAKER. Very well. Divine Caesar, I have come here with my army to subjugate myself and all the Goths to you.

(OTTAKER *drops to his knees, presenting sword-hilt to* ROMULUS.)

Take my sword. I surrender.

ROMULUS. Surrender! You're out of your mind! Here! Stop that! Get up this minute. I don't want your sword.

OTTAKER. Because I am Gothic does not mean that I cannot be led by intelligence.

ROMULUS. But this is all wrong. This *can't* happen! For Heaven's sake, get up off that floor.

OTTAKER (*rising*). We have discussed chickens intelligently. Agreed?

ROMULUS. Agreed.

OTTAKER. Then why can't we discuss our two countries intelligently?

ROMULUS. Because it is not done.

OTTAKER. May I sit, Divine Caesar?

ROMULUS. I don't find that at all amusing. Of course you may sit. You are the conqueror, I am the conquered.

(OTTAKER *sits at the table.*)

OTTAKER. That was a moment ago. Since then I surrendered to you.

ROMULUS. If only my poor wife could see me now! I who baffled everyone for twenty years am now completely mystified by a Goth. Go right ahead. Sit down. Have some asparagus wine. No, that's right, you don't like it. I'm afraid we have no beer. Have an egg.

OTTAKER. I am perfectly serious.

ROMULUS. So am I when I say that you must kill me.

OTTAKER. Why?

ROMULUS. Because that is my fate. Because that is the way I have planned it.

OTTAKER. You are not God.

ROMULUS. No. But ... curious, my wife said the same thing.

OTTAKER. Why are you so eager to die?

ROMULUS. I am not eager only ... (*Stops; begins again.*) Ottaker, when I was young I looked about me and I saw an old world crumbling, this world. On every side I saw forms without use, prayers without faith, laws without justice. And I said to myself: This must come to an end. But not in the usual, gradual, deadly way, but all at once. *I* would bring it down. And in its fall men might see a lesson. See justice for once on earth give perfect measure.

OTTAKER. Perfect justice? There is no such thing.

ROMULUS. Just before you arrived, I was told that my daughter was dead, because of me. But I did not weep. Because I knew that I would die, too. I myself would expiate Rome's sins. Now you propose to rob me of my fate? Of my duty? No. Not even the Gothic Butcher could be that cruel.

OTTAKER. Your grief will pass.

(ROMULUS *picks up the sword at his feet.*)

ROMULUS. You are afraid. Now then, conquer your fear. Do it!

(ROMULUS *tries to force the sword on* OTTAKER.)

OTTAKER (*turns away*). I cannot kill you.

ROMULUS. I must say your reputation as a butcher is quite undeserved.

OTTAKER. Have you any idea what will happen to me if you refuse to become our leader?

ROMULUS. Yes. You will be known as the man who conquered the world. Ottaker the Great. You will be much admired.

OTTAKER. No. I shall be murdered.

ROMULUS. Well, that is an occupational hazard, to be taken in stride.

OTTAKER. The oracles all agree that one day Theodoric will say: *No,* dear Uncle. And that will be the end of me.

ROMULUS. I never interfere in family matters.

OTTAKER. And when I'm gone, Theodoric will build a new Rome. More monstrous, more terrible than the old. And you will have sacrificed yourself for nothing.

ROMULUS. I am interested in the past, not the future. In moral example, not in political demonstration.

OTTAKER. Romulus, save me.

ROMULUS. Certainly not.

OTTAKER. Then save the human race from Theodoric.

ROMULUS. My work is done. Now, in the name of Heaven, will you complete this farce?

OTTAKER. Certainly not.

(ROMULUS *drops the sword.*)

ROMULUS. All right. I shall fetch Titus. He is in the garden. He'll do it.

(ROMULUS *starts toward the garden.*)

OTTAKER. Stop!

(ROMULUS *stops; he turns, smiling.*)

ROMULUS. You are master here ... you see?

OTTAKER (*grimly*). All right. You force me to rule. I shall force you to live.

ROMULUS. But if I live, my life has been a failure.

OTTAKER. Let me be the judge of that. If the world was as you thought it was, your remarkable experiment might have had some point. But the world is not neat. The world is not a book. Life is a river, a flood. You cannot change its course. You were not there at its beginning. You will not be there at its end. So live, Caesar.

ROMULUS. Live? Now? The work of twenty years come to nothing? No!

OTTAKER. You insist upon being classical, don't you? (*Takes sword.*) Then I shall be classic, too. I shall begin my new reign with a murder.

ROMULUS. What murder?

OTTAKER. I shall do to Theodoric what he plans to do to me.

ROMULUS. Stop! That would be foolish.

OTTAKER. Foolish? Necessary.

ROMULUS. Better the enemy you know than a thousand you do not. You can keep an eye on one, but not on many.

OTTAKER. Then you *are* interested in what becomes of me? That means you are interested in life. Good.

ROMULUS. You weren't going to kill him, were you? It was a trick.

OTTAKER. Not entirely. Theodoric does mean to have my head.

ROMULUS. But perhaps he won't get it. The future is most unreliable – as I have discovered. There is no way of controlling it.

(OTTAKER *sees his opportunity.*)

OTTAKER. Do you mean to say that I cannot judge the future?

ROMULUS. No one can judge the future.

OTTAKER (*almost casually*). Then can anyone judge the past?

ROMULUS. No one can judge ... (*He stops, stricken*). Oh, God! (*He sits, heavily.*) I sacrificed what was left of Rome because I hated its past. You were willing to sacrifice your Goths ...

OTTAKER. Because I fear their future.

ROMULUS. Yet if you were really afraid, why did you conquer the world? Why did you murder thousands of men and women in the name of ... nothing?

OTTAKER. Public opinion. Theodoric wanted war. He convinced my people *they* wanted war. They forced *me* to mobilize. I thought if I took charge of the army, we could at least have a humane war.

ROMULUS. You were naive.

OTTAKER. I know that now. My army has been brutal. Cruel. No worse than any other army, but even so I've been shocked by what we've done. I tried to quit. I was willing to accept that fellow's offer ... what's his name ... makes pants?

ROMULUS. Otto Rupf. Who will, I promise you, inherit the earth.

OTTAKER. Yes. I thought I could bribe my officers while they were still corruptible. But the closer we came to the city of Rome, the more they believed in Gothic-ism.

ROMULUS. Which is nothing.

OTTAKER. Which is nothing.

ROMULUS. Yet you have no power over the future. I had no power over the past.

OTTAKER (*blackly*). And now time has us by the throat.

ROMULUS. There is only one thing left.

OTTAKER. There is nothing left.

ROMULUS. But there is. The present. The day. The moment. The instant. *Now*.

OTTAKER. Go on ...

ROMULUS. Given the present ... and the two of us ... here ... in this room, there is a great deal we can do.

OTTAKER. Name it!

ROMULUS. First, a treaty of peace.

OTTAKER. The terms?

ROMULUS. Well, I might make you Emperor of Rome ...

OTTAKER. No. No. *You* are the last Emperor.

ROMULUS. Oh, yes. That's right. We mustn't rob me of my one small distinction. I've worked very hard to be the last. Then I shall make you *King* of Italy. How's that?

OTTAKER. But how long will I reign? How long before Theodoric ...

ROMULUS. The present ... remember? The past is a dream. The future does not exist. Since we cannot have perfection, we must make do with imperfection.

OTTAKER. We are human.

ROMULUS. We are human.

OTTAKER. And there are no absolutes?

ROMULUS. No absolutes. Only the long present ... the now. So let us begin, Ottaker, to live now.

OTTAKER. Without great expectations.

ROMULUS. But without despair.

OTTAKER. The conditions of the peace treaty?

ROMULUS. The simplest. You and I – two mistaken men who came to their senses – we will make it safe to breed chickens from one end of Europe to the other. Historians will snub us, of course. Not enough battles. But ours is the true glory.

OTTAKER. Brief glory.

ROMULUS. But make the moment good and who knows what will come?

OTTAKER. I am a pessimist. But I will be led by you.

(*Both rise.*)

ROMULUS. And now let us, as sovereigns, act as if all the accounts in the world were finally balanced, as though spirit had finally triumphed over matter.

OTTAKER (*shouts*). Nephew!

(THEODORIC *enters, carrying a pike.*)

THEODORIC. Yes, dear Uncle?

OTTAKER. Summon the chiefs of staff.

THEODORIC. But, dear Uncle ...

(OTTAKER *looks at* ROMULUS *with mock alarm.*)

OTTAKER. What did he say?

ROMULUS. I believe he said, "*But,* dear Uncle."

OTTAKER. That's what I thought he said. (*Turns to his nephew.*) Yes, Theodoric?

THEODORIC. Here is the pike.

OTTAKER. So?

THEODORIC (*indicates* ROMULUS). But there is his head.

OTTAKER. Naturally.

THEODORIC. His head should be *on* the pike.

ROMULUS. I'm sorry. I did my best to put it there for you.

THEODORIC. Dear Uncle, we *must* have his head. We owe it to our people. We owe it to Gothic-ism.

OTTAKER. Nephew: What are the four great virtues of Gothic-ism?

THEODORIC (*comes to attention*). Perfect courage. Absolute sincerity. Complete faith. Total obedience.

OTTAKER. Then, Nephew, be perfectly courageous. Accept things the way they are. Be absolutely sincere. Do not plot against me. Have complete faith. That all things are for the best. Be totally obedient ... (*Bellows.*) *and summon the chiefs of staff!*

THEODORIC (*frightened*). Yes, dear Uncle. (*He runs off stage right.*)

ROMULUS. Very impressive, Ottaker. You handled that well. (*Frowns.*) But aren't you afraid that one day he might ...

OTTAKER (*quickly*). The present. Remember?

ROMULUS (*smiles*). You are a good student. (*A deep breath.*) What an odd feeling to be alive! I'd quite got used to death.

OTTAKER (*nods*). It's a pleasant feeling, life.

ROMULUS. Yes. I'd almost forgotten. We must *never* forget that. In fact, I shall write it down this very minute. "Life is good." If I can find a piece of paper.

(OTTO RUPF, PYRAMUS *and* ACHILLES *enter, all in trousers.*)

ROMULUS. Ah, Mr. Rupf, how reassuring to see you on the job.

RUPF. The early bird gets the worm.

ROMULUS. Organically speaking.

(*The* GOTHIC SOLDIERS *enter. They are in field uniform, worn and dusty.*)

OTTAKER (*resonantly*). Goths! Dusty, tired, burned by the sun, your duty is done at last. Gothic-ism has triumphed!

(*Three cheers: "All hail! All hail! All hail!"* OTTAKER *and* ROMULUS *exchange glances.*)

Before you sits Romulus, the Emperor of Rome. Salute him.

(*The* MEN *salute.*)

There he is. The man you mocked. The man you sang your songs about. The enemy of Gothic-ism. Yet I have come to know his quality. His greatness. You will never see his like again. You will never see a greater man, no matter *who* my successor is.

(THEODORIC *looks at* OTTAKER, *startled.* OTTAKER *looks at him challengingly.* THEODORIC *snaps to attention.* ROMULUS *rises.*)

ROMULUS. Thank you for that generous introduction. And now, watch while the Emperor of Rome dissolves his Empire. (*With his hand he designates an imaginary globe.*) For the last time look upon this great world, floating in air, set spinning by the breath from my lips. Look upon those green and fertile lands set in the blue sea, with its dolphins and sudden storms. Rich provinces yellow with grain. Tall cities swarming with life. (*He starts to contract the globe.*) Look upon this Rome, this sun which at its zenith consumed the earth with fire ... now a toy in my hand (*He closes his hand.*) which I let drop (*He opens hand, palm down.*) and vanish into nothing.

(*There is a long moment of silence. The* GOTHS *are mystified.* ROMULUS *takes sword from table.*)

ROMULUS (*briskly*). Ottaker, Prince of the Goths, I name you King of Italy.

(ROMULUS *gives* OTTAKER *the sword.*)

OTTAKER. For my part, I grant Romulus the villa of Lucullus. As well as a pension of six thousand gold pieces a year.

ROMULUS (*smiles*). The lean years have ended. Oh! The laurel wreath. (*Removes wreath.*) What's left of it. It goes with your new position. (*He places wreath on* OTTAKER'*s head.*) You are now King. Such is the will of the Senate and the people of Rome. SPQR. You will find the Senate, if you want them, in the Catacombs. They will come out if you grant them unlimited debate. I always did. Talking keeps them out of mischief. You will find the people of Rome going about their usual business. Tell them you're in charge now. They will hardly notice the difference.

(ROMULUS *crosses to table.*)

Goodbye, Ottaker. Be a good king.

OTTAKER (*amused*). I shall try.

(ROMULUS *takes a last sip of wine.*)

ROMULUS. The present is all that we have. Make it good.

(OTTAKER *suddenly salutes him.*)

OTTAKER. Hail, Romulus the Great!

GOTHS (*in unison*). Hail, Romulus the Great!

(TITUS *rushes on stage from left, his sword drawn.*)

TITUS. Down with the Emperor! Where is he? Let me kill him! Where is the Emperor?

(OTTAKER *steps between* TITUS *and* ROMULUS.)

OTTAKER. Put down that sword. There is no Emperor.

TITUS. No Emperor. (*Points to* ROMULUS.) But there he is.

OTTAKER. That is a chicken breeder from Campania. The Empire was dissolved some minutes ago.

TITUS (*stunned.*) Rome ... gone?

ROMULUS (*softly*). I'm afraid so. All gone. It was only a dream, as you suspected. (*Smiles.*) Anyway, you finally got your rest.

TITUS (*slowly*). And so the last Roman soldier slept through the end of his world.

(TITUS, *shattered, sits in the Emperor's chair, face in his hands.*)

ROMULUS. And on that ... wistful note, gentlemen, the Roman Empire is at an end.

(ROMULUS *slowly walks off stage right as the* GOTHS *watch in awe and wonder. The rooster crows.*)

ROMULUS THE GREAT

by Friedrich Duerrenmatt

An Historical Comedy Without Historic Basis

Second Version 1957

> The great artistic trick of taking small deviations from the truth for truth itself upon which the entire system of differential equations is built, is also the basis for our wittiest thinking which might all collapse if the deviations were taken with philosophical strictness.
>
> LICHTENBERG

CHARACTERS

ROMULUS AUGUSTUS	Emperor of the Western Roman Empire
JULIA	His Wife
REA	His Daughter
ZENO, THE ISAURIAN	Emperor of the Eastern Roman Empire
EMILIAN	Roman Patrician
MARES	Minister of War
TULLIUS ROTUNDUS	Minister of State
SPURIUS TITUS MAMMA	Captain of Cavalry
ACHILLES	Chamberlain to Romulus
PYRAMUS	Chamberlain to Romulus
APOLLONIUS	Antique Dealer
CAESAR RUPF	Industrialist
PHYLAX	Actor
ODOAKER	Ruler of the Teutons
THEODORIC	His Nephew
PHOSPHORIDES	Chamberlain to Zeno
SULPHURIDES	Chamberlain to Zeno
COOK, PORTERS, TEUTONS	

The Time: The morning of March 15th to the morning of March 16th, A.D. 476.

The Place: The Country Residence of Emperor Romulus.

ACT ONE

It is the year four hundred and seventy-six. One early March morning the Cavalry officer, SPURIUS TITUS MAMMA, *arrives on his dying horse in Campania at the imperial summer residence in which the Emperor of Rome lives the whole year round. The* CAPTAIN, *soiled and with his left arm in a bloody bandage, dismounts, moving with difficulty; he stumbles, stirring up a huge flock of cackling chickens; hurries, finding no one, through the villa and finally enters the Emperor's study. Here, too, everything seems to him at first empty and deserted. There are a few wobbly, half-broken chairs and up on the walls the venerable busts of Rome's statesmen, thinkers and poets, all of a somewhat exaggeratedly solemn mien …*

SPURIUS TITUS MAMMA. Hallo, hallo, anybody here?

(*Silence. At last the* CAVALRY OFFICER *notices two ancient, grey and immovable chamberlains, standing like statues, at each side of a door in the middle of the background.* PYRAMUS *and* ACHILLES *have been in the service of the Emperor for years. The* CAVALRY OFFICER *stares at them in amazement and, impressed by their dignified appearance, becomes quite timid.*)

Hallo!

PYRAMUS. Silence, young man.

SPURIUS TITUS MAMMA. It's about time. I was beginning to think this place was dead to the world. I am dog-tired.

(*Panting for breath, he throws himself into a chair.*)

ACHILLES. And who are you?

SPURIUS TITUS MAMMA. Spurius Titus Mamma, Captain of Cavalry.

PYRAMUS. And what do you want?

SPURIUS TITUS MAMMA. I have to speak to the Emperor.

ACHILLES. Have you an appointment?

SPURIUS TITUS MAMMA. No time for formalities. I bring urgent news.

PYRAMUS. Nothing is urgent at the Court of a Roman Emperor, Spurius Titus Mamma.

(*The* CAPTAIN *jumps up angrily.*)

SPURIUS TITUS MAMMA. But I come from Pavia, from the Imperial Commander, Orestes, with bad news!

(*The two chamberlains look at each other thoughtfully.*)

PYRAMUS. Bad news from Pavia?

ACHILLES (*shakes his head*). News from Pavia cannot really be bad. Pavia is too insignificant for that!

SPURIUS TITUS MAMMA. But the Roman Empire is collapsing!

(*He is simply speechless at the composure of the two chamberlains.*)

PYRAMUS. Impossible.

ACHILLES. An organization as immense as the Roman Empire simply cannot totally collapse.

SPURIUS TITUS MAMMA. But the Teutons are coming.

ACHILLES. They have been coming for the past five hundred years, Spurius Titus Mamma.

(*The* CAVALRY OFFICER *grabs* ACHILLES *by the shoulders and shakes him as if he were a rotten column.*)

SPURIUS TITUS MAMMA. As a patriot, it is my duty to speak to the Emperor! At once!

ACHILLES. Patriotism which conflicts with cultivated behaviour is undesirable.

SPURIUS TITUS MAMMA. For the love of the gods!

(*Discouraged, he lets go of* ACHILLES *and now* PYRAMUS *tries to appease him.*)

PYRAMUS. Let me give you some good advice, young man. Take it and you will gain your objective swiftly. First go to the Lord High Steward. At ten o'clock sharp, two hours from now, he will hold audience. Add your name to the list of new arrivals. Request permission from the Minister of State to deliver an important message to the Imperial Court and perhaps then, in the course of the next few days, you may be able to deliver your news personally to the Emperor.

(*The* CAVALRY OFFICER *no longer knows what to think.*)

SPURIUS TITUS MAMMA. To the Lord High Steward!

PYRAMUS. Right round the corner, third door on the left.

SPURIUS TITUS MAMMA. To the Minister of State!

PYRAMUS. Seventh door on the right.

SPURIUS TITUS MAMMA (*still speechless*). To deliver my news in the course of the next few days!

ACHILLES. In the course of the next few weeks.

SPURIUS TITUS MAMMA. Unhappy Rome! Two chamberlains are your downfall! (*He runs desperately out to the left. The two chamberlains again freeze into immobility.*)

ACHILLES. Most regrettably I note that as our century progresses, its manners decline.

PYRAMUS. He who misjudges our worth digs Rome's grave.

(*The* EMPEROR, ROMULUS AUGUSTUS, *appears in the door where the chamberlains are standing. He is wearing a purple toga and a golden wreath. His Majesty is past fifty, calm, at ease and sure of himself.*)

PYRAMUS AND ACHILLES. Hail, Caesar.

ROMULUS. Hail. Are today the Ides of March?

ACHILLES. Yes, my Emperor, the Ides of March. (*He bows.*)

ROMULUS. An historic date. According to Roman Law all officials and civil servants of my empire are to be paid today. An ancient rite to keep emperors from being assassinated. Get me the Minister of Finance.

ACHILLES. The Minister of Finance has fled, my Emperor.

ROMULUS. Fled?

PYRAMUS. With the imperial cash-box.

ROMULUS. Why? There was nothing in it.

ACHILLES. He did it in the hope of covering up the general bankruptcy of the imperial finances.

ROMULUS. Clever, that man. If you want to hide a great scandal, it's best to stage a little one. Let him henceforth be called 'The Saviour of his Country'. Where is he now?

ACHILLES. They say in Syracuse – as head clerk of a wine export business.

ROMULUS. Let us hope that in business this loyal official will succeed in recovering the losses he incurred serving the state. Let's see now! (*He takes his wreath off his head, breaks off two golden leaves and hands one to each of the chamberlains.*) Let each of you turn his golden leaf into sesterces. But after deducting what I owe you, give me back any money left. I still have to pay my cook; he's the most important man in my empire.

PYRAMUS AND ACHILLES. Yes, Your Majesty.

ROMULUS. When I began to reign there were thirty-six leaves in my wreath, this symbol of imperial power. Now there are only five. (*Thoughtfully he looks at the wreath before putting it back on.*) My morning repast.

PYRAMUS. Your breakfast.

ROMULUS. My morning repast. In my house I decide what is classical Latin.

(*The old man brings in a small table; on it stands the* EMPEROR*'s breakfast. There is ham, bread, asparagus wine, a small bowl of milk, an egg in its cup.* ACHILLES *brings in a chair. The* EMPEROR *sits down and opens the egg.*)

ROMULUS. Did Augustus lay?

PYRAMUS. No, my Emperor.

ROMULUS. Tiberius?

PYRAMUS. Julian, nothing.

ROMULUS. Flavius?

PYRAMUS. Domitian did, but Your Majesty expressly did not wish to eat even one of Domitian's eggs.

ROMULUS. Domitian was a bad emperor. No matter how many eggs that bird lays, I shall not eat them.

PYRAMUS. Yes, my Emperor.

(*The* EMPEROR *eats up the egg.*)

ROMULUS. And who laid this egg?

PYRAMUS. Marcus Aurelius, as usual.

ROMULUS. A fine bird. Compared to him, the other emperors are worthless. Did anybody else lay anything?

PYRAMUS. Odoaker. (*He is somewhat embarrassed.*)

ROMULUS. I declare!

PYRAMUS. Two eggs.

ROMULUS. Marvellous. And Orestes, my Commander-in-Chief, who is supposed to conquer this Teutonic chieftain?

PYRAMUS. Nothing.

ROMULUS. Nothing? I never did think much of him. Let that one be served for supper tonight, stuffed with chestnuts.

PYRAMUS. Yes, Your Majesty.

(*The* EMPEROR *eats ham and bread.*)

ROMULUS. And what news of the bird bearing my name?

PYRAMUS. She is the noblest, most gifted fowl we possess, the blue-ribbon product of Roman poultry raising.

ROMULUS. Did she lay, this noble bird?

(PYRAMUS *looks at* ACHILLES, *pleading for help.*)

ACHILLES. Almost, my Emperor.

ROMULUS. Almost? What does that mean? A hen either lays or she does not.

ACHILLES. Not yet, my Emperor.

(*The* EMPEROR *makes a decisive gesture.*)

ROMULUS. If a hen lays not, she's still good for the pot. Let the cook prepare my namesake along with Orestes and Caligula.

PYRAMUS. But, Your Majesty, the day before yesterday you ate Caligula together with Philippus Arabus, served with asparagus.

ROMULUS. Then let him take my predecessor, Julius Nepos. He was not good for anything either. And in future, I desire that the eggs of the hen Odoaker be served for my morning repast. This fine animal has my fullest admiration. What enormous talent. Let us take from the Teutons whatever good they produce; they seem to be coming anyhow.

(*The Minister of State,* TULLIUS ROTUNDUS, *pale as death, rushes in from the left.*)

TULLIUS ROTUNDUS. My Emperor!

ROMULUS. What do you wish of your Emperor, Tullius Rotundus?

TULLIUS ROTUNDUS. It is terrible, simply frightful.

ROMULUS. I know, my dear Minister. For two years now I have not paid you, and today, when I meant to do it, the Minister of Finance ran away with the imperial cash-box.

TULLIUS ROTUNDUS. Our position is so catastrophic that nobody, but nobody, thinks of money any more, my Emperor.

(*The* EMPEROR *drinks his bowl of milk.*)

ROMULUS. Well, I am in luck again.

TULLIUS ROTUNDUS. A cavalry captain, Spurius Titus Mamma, rode his horse at the gallop two days and two nights to bring Your Majesty news from Pavia.

ROMULUS. Two days and two nights! Now that is really something. He shall be made a Centurion for his athletic prowess.

TULLIUS ROTUNDUS. I will lead the Centurion, Spurius Titus Mamma, to Your Majesty right away.

ROMULUS. But, my dear Minister of State, isn't he tired?

TULLIUS ROTUNDUS. Of course, he is exhausted in mind and body.

ROMULUS. In that case, my dear Tullius Rotundus, you had better lead him to the quietest guest chamber in my house. Even athletes must sleep.

(*The* MINISTER OF STATE *is taken aback.*)

TULLIUS ROTUNDUS. But his news, Your Majesty.

ROMULUS. Precisely. Even the worst news sounds quite acceptable from the mouth of a person who is well rested, freshly bathed, shaved, and well fed. Let him come tomorrow.

(*The* MINISTER OF STATE *is speechless.*)

TULLIUS ROTUNDUS. Your Majesty! But this is world-shaking news.

ROMULUS. News never shakes the world. Events do that, but

once we get news of them, they're past altering. News only agitates the world: it's best to do without news.

(TULLIUS ROTUNDUS *bows in confusion and goes off to the left.* PYRAMUS *sets a large joint of roast beef before* ROMULUS.)

ACHILLES. The art dealer, Apollonius.

(APOLLONIUS, *the art dealer, enters from the left. He is dressed elegantly in the Greek manner. He bows.*)

APOLLONIUS. My Emperor.

ROMULUS. For three weeks I have been waiting for you.

APOLLONIUS. I beg your forgiveness, my Emperor. I have been at an auction in Alexandria.

ROMULUS. You prefer an auction in Alexandria to the meeting of creditors of the Roman Empire?

APOLLONIUS. Business is business, my Emperor.

ROMULUS. Well, were you not delighted with the busts I sold you? Cicero, especially, was a valuable piece.

APOLLONIUS. An exception, my Emperor. I was able to send off five hundred plaster casts to the academies which are being founded everywhere in the ancient Teutonic forests.

ROMULUS. For heaven's sake, Apollonius, is Germania being civilized?

APOLLONIUS. The light of reason cannot be stopped. When the Teutons become civilized at home, they will no longer invade the Roman Empire.

(*The* EMPEROR *carves the beef.*)

ROMULUS. When the Teutons come to Italia or Gaul, we will civilize them. But if they remain in Germania, they will civilize themselves and that will be ghastly. Do you wish to buy the remaining busts or not?

(*The art dealer looks around.*)

APOLLONIUS. I had better look them over once more. There is little call for busts these days; quite frankly, the only ones that sell are those of famous pugilists and buxom courtesans. Besides, some of these busts seem of rather dubious style.

ROMULUS. Each bust has the style it deserves. Achilles, hand Apollonius a ladder.

(ACHILLES *hands a ladder to the art dealer. The Greek climbs the ladder and keeps himself occupied examining the busts, now climbing up the ladder, now down, moving the ladder from place to place. The* EMPRESS JULIA *enters from the right.*)

JULIA. Romulus.

ROMULUS. My dear wife.

JULIA. How can you eat at a time like this?

(*The* EMPEROR *puts down his knife and fork.*)

ROMULUS. As you wish, my dear Julia.

JULIA. I'm deeply troubled, Romulus. The Lord High Steward, Ebius, gave me to understand that we have had terrible news. Now I don't quite always believe Ebius, since he is a Teuton and his real name is Ebi –

ROMULUS. Ebius is the only man fluent in all five world-languages: Latin, Greek, Hebrew, German, and Chinese, though I must admit German sounds Chinese to me. But no matter, Ebius is better educated than any Roman will ever be.

JULIA. You are a real Germanophile, Romulus.

ROMULUS. Nonsense. I do not like them half as much as I like my chickens.

JULIA. Romulus!

ROMULUS. Pyramus, set a place for the Empress and bring Odoaker's first egg.

JULIA. Remember my weak heart!

ROMULUS. Precisely. Sit down and eat.

(*The* EMPRESS *sits down at the left of the table with a sigh.*)

JULIA. Now will you tell me at last what terrible news came this morning?

ROMULUS. I don't know. The courier who brought it is sleeping.

JULIA. Then have him awakened, Romulus!

ROMULUS. Think of your heart, my dear wife.

JULIA. As the mother of my country ...

ROMULUS. As the father of my country, I will probably be

Rome's last emperor. For that reason alone, I occupy a rather forlorn position in world history. No matter what happens I shall end up with a bad reputation. But there is one bit of fame no one shall take from me: no one shall ever say that I had wilfully disturbed the sleep of any man unnecessarily.

(*The* PRINCESS REA *enters from the right.*)

REA. Good day, Father.

ROMULUS. Good day, dear daughter.

REA. Did you sleep well?

ROMULUS. Since I am the Emperor I always sleep well.

(REA *sits down at the right of the table.*)

ROMULUS. Pyramus, set a place for the Princess, too, and bring Odoaker's second egg.

REA. Oh, did Odoaker lay two eggs today?

ROMULUS. These Teutons are highly productive. Would you like some ham?

REA. No, thank you.

ROMULUS. Cold roast beef?

REA. No, thank you.

ROMULUS. A little fish?

REA. No, thank you.

ROMULUS. Some asparagus wine?

(*He frowns.*)

REA. No, thank you, Father.

ROMULUS. Ever since you have been taking dramatic lessons from this actor, Phylax, you have no appetite. Just what are you studying?

REA. Antigone's elegy before her death.

ROMULUS. Why study that old tragic text? Why not comedy? It's more fitting for our time.

(*The* EMPRESS *is enraged.*)

JULIA. Romulus, you know very well this would not be fitting for a young maiden whose betrothed has been languishing for more than three years in a Teutonic dungeon.

ROMULUS. Calm yourself, my dear wife; people whose number is up, like us, can only understand comedy.

ACHILLES. His Excellency, the Minister of War, wishes to speak to His Majesty. He says it is urgent.

ROMULUS. Strange, but the Minister of War always comes when I am discussing literature. Let him come after my morning repast.

JULIA. Will you tell the Minister that the Emperor's family will be delighted to see him, Achilles.

(ACHILLES *bows and goes off to the left. The* EMPEROR *wipes his mouth with his napkin.*)

ROMULUS. You are being excessively martial again, my dear wife.

(*The* MINISTER OF WAR *enters, bowing, from the left.*)

MARES. My Emperor.

ROMULUS. Odd, how pale all my officials are today. I had noticed it earlier in the Minister of State. What do you wish, Mares?

MARES. As the Minister responsible for the conduct of the war against the Teutons, I must demand that Your Majesty receive the Captain of Cavalry, Spurius Titus Mamma, now.

ROMULUS. But isn't our athlete asleep yet?

MARES. It is unworthy of a soldier to sleep when he knows his Emperor is in need.

ROMULUS. My officers' sense of duty is beginning to annoy me.

(*The* EMPRESS *rises.*)

JULIA. Romulus!

ROMULUS. My dearest Julia?

JULIA. You are going to receive Spurius Titus Mamma immediately.

(PYRAMUS *whispers something into the* EMPEROR*'s ear.*)

ROMULUS. That is quite unnecessary, my dear wife. Pyramus just now announced that Odoaker has laid a third egg.

JULIA. Romulus, your empire is tottering, your soldiers are sacrificing themselves and you do nothing but speak of your feathered flock!

ROMULUS. Precisely. And this is entirely legitimate ever since the geese saved the Capitol. I no longer need Spurius Titus Mamma. The ruler of the Teutons, Odoaker, has conquered Pavia. I know this is so because the hen bearing his name has just laid three eggs, and all things come in threes. You see how it all fits; without this natural harmony, there would be no order in the world.

(*Great consternation.*)

REA. My dear Father!

JULIA. That cannot be true.

MARES. Unfortunately, it is the truth, Your Majesty. Pavia has fallen. Rome has suffered the bitterest defeat of its history. The captain brought us the last words of the Commander, Orestes. He and his entire army fell into Teutonic hands.

ROMULUS. I know the last words of my generals even before they fall into Teutonic hands: As long as there is a drop of blood in our veins, no one will give up. Every one of them said that. Now, my dear Minister of War, will you please go and tell the Centurion of Cavalry that he is to go to bed.

(MARES *bows in silence and goes off to the left.*)

JULIA. You must do something, Romulus. You must do something immediately or else we shall be lost!

ROMULUS. This afternoon I will issue a proclamation to my soldiers.

JULIA. Your legions, to the very last man, have deserted to the Teutons.

ROMULUS. In that case I will proclaim Mares, Imperial Marshal.

JULIA. Mares is a silly fool.

ROMULUS. Precisely. There is not a sensible man left today who would become Minister of War of the Roman Empire. I will issue a communiqué that I am in good health.

JULIA. What good will that do?

ROMULUS. I'm reigning as always. You cannot possibly ask more of me than that, my dear wife.

(APOLLONIUS, *who has been busy looking at busts, descends*

from his ladder, approaches the EMPEROR *and shows him a bust.*)

APOLLONIUS. Three gold pieces for this Ovid, my Emperor.

ROMULUS. Four pieces. Ovid was a great poet.

JULIA. And who is this, Romulus?

ROMULUS. The art dealer Apollonius, from Syracuse. I am selling him my busts.

JULIA. But you cannot possibly squander the famous poets, thinkers, and statesmen of Rome's great past!

ROMULUS. We are having a closing-down sale.

JULIA. Do bear in mind that these busts are the only things my father, Valentian, left you.

ROMULUS. But I still have you, my dear wife.

REA. I simply cannot stand it any more.

(*She rises.*)

JULIA. Rea!

REA. I'm going to study Antigone.

(*She goes off to the right.*)

JULIA. You see, even your daughter no longer understands you!

ROMULUS. That's only because of her drama lessons.

APOLLONIUS. Three gold pieces and six sesterces. My final offer, Your Majesty.

ROMULUS. Why don't you take a few more busts? Then we will settle the whole thing in a lump sum.

(APOLLONIUS *starts climbing up his ladder again. The* MINISTER OF STATE *rushes in from the left.*)

TULLIUS ROTUNDUS. My Emperor!

ROMULUS. Now what do you want, Tullius Rotundus?

TULLIUS ROTUNDUS. Zeno the Isaurian, Emperor of East Rome, begs for asylum.

ROMULUS. Zeno the Isaurian? But is he not safe in Constantinople?

TULLIUS ROTUNDUS. No one is safe in this world any more.

ROMULUS. Well, where is he?

TULLIUS ROTUNDUS. In the ante-room.

ROMULUS. Did he bring along his chamberlains, Sulphurides and Phosphoridos?

TULLIUS ROTUNDUS. They were the only ones who could flee with him.

ROMULUS. If he will leave Sulphurides and Phosphoridos outside, then Zeno may come in. Byzantine chamberlains are too strict to suit me.

TULLIUS ROTUNDUS. Very well, Your Majesty.

(The EMPEROR ZENO, *the Isaurian, rushes in from the left. He is dressed considerably more expensively and more elegantly than his West Roman colleague.)*

ZENO. Hail to you, my exalted Imperial Brother!

ROMULUS. Hail to you.

ZENO. Hail to you, exalted Imperial Sister!

JULIA. Hail to you, exalted Imperial Brother!

(They all embrace. ZENO *strikes the attitude of an East Roman emperor seeking political asylum.)*

ZENO. I plead for help.

ROMULUS. I won't insist on your reciting all the numerous verses the Byzantine ceremonial demands of an emperor seeking asylum, my dear Zeno.

ZENO. I cannot cheat my chamberlains.

ROMULUS. But if I will not let them in?

ZENO. Well, in that case, I won't recite the prescribed formalities this time, that is as long as my chamberlains don't see. I'm exhausted. Ever since we left Constantinople they've made me recite the innumerable verses of 'I plead for help' at least three times a day in front of all sorts of political personalities. My voice is simply ruined.

ROMULUS. Sit down.

ZENO. Thank you.

(Relieved, he sits down at the table, but at that very moment his two CHAMBERLAINS *rush in, both dressed in severe black clothes.)*

THE TWO CHAMBERLAINS. Your Majesty!

ZENO. By Zeus! How did my chamberlains manage to get in?

SULPHURIDES. Your elegiac verses, Your Majesty.

ZENO. I have already recited them, my dear Sulphurides and Phosphoridos.

SULPHURIDES. Impossible, Your Majesty. I appeal to your pride. You are not some private person running away. You are the East Roman Emperor in emigration and as such you must submit gladly to all the ceremonial rules of the Byzantine Court, no matter how incomprehensible they may be. Now, if you please?

ZENO. If it absolutely has to be?

PHOSPHORIDES. It has to be, Your Majesty. The Byzantine Court ceremonial is not only a symbol of world order, indeed it is the world order itself. You should have understood that a long time ago. Commence, Your Majesty. Do not shame your chamberlains any longer.

ZENO. But I'm going to.

SULPHURIDES. Step back three paces, Your Majesty.

PHOSPHORIDOS. On your knees, with head bent, Your Majesty.

ZENO. Pleading mercy, I approach you. May the moon ...

PHOSPHORIDOS. The sun.

ROMULUS. Achilles! Pyramus!

PYRAMUS. Yes, Majesty?

ACHILLES. Your Majesty?

ROMULUS. Throw out those two Byzantine chamberlains and lock them up in the chicken yard.

ACHILLES. Very well, my Emperor.

SULPHURIDES. We protest!

PHOSPHORIDOS. Respectfully but emphatically!

(*At last the two are pushed out of the door by* ACHILLES *and* PYRAMUS; *they disappear with* ACHILLES. PYRAMUS *exhaustedly wipes the sweat off his brow.*)

ZENO. The gods be thanked, my chamberlains are gone. Under their mountain of formalities and rules they bury me alive. I must walk according to style, speak according to style, even eat and drink according to style. I cannot stand all that style.

But the moment they're gone I feel the ancient strength of my Isaurian forefathers rise in me. The old faith, firm as a rock – is the fence to your chicken yard good and firm?

ROMULUS. You can depend on it. Pyramus, set a place for Zeno and bring an egg.

PYRAMUS. But we only have Domitian's egg.

ROMULUS. In this case it will do.

ZENO (*embarrassed*). As a matter of fact, you know, you and I have been at war these past seven years. Only the common Teutonic menace kept our armies from any major engagements.

ROMULUS. We? At war? I didn't know that.

ZENO. But I took Dalmatia from you.

ROMULUS. Did it ever belong to me?

ZENO. At the last division of the empire it was assigned to you.

ROMULUS. Speaking between us emperors, it has been quite some time since I've had a comprehensive view of world politics. Why did you have to leave Constantinople?

ZENO. Verina, my mother-in-law, formed an alliance with the Teutons and drove me out.

ROMULUS. Odd. And you have such excellent relations with the Teutons.

ZENO. Romulus! (*His feelings are hurt.*)

ROMULUS. You had entered into an alliance with them in order to depose your own son as emperor – if my information about the complicated situation at the Byzantine Court is correct.

JULIA. Romulus!

ZENO. The Teutons are overrunning our empires. All our defences have been more or less breached. We can no longer march separately. We cannot afford the luxury of petty suspicions between our two empires. We must save our culture.

ROMULUS. Why? Is culture something anyone can save?

JULIA. Romulus!

(*In the meantime the antique dealer has approached the* EMPEROR *with several busts.*)

APOLLONIUS. For the two Gracchi, Pompeius, Scipio, and Cato, two gold pieces and eight sesterces.

ROMULUS. Three gold pieces.

APOLLONIUS. All right, but in that case I will take Marius and Scilla also.

(*He climbs back up the ladder.*)

JULIA. Romulus, I demand that you send this antique dealer away immediately.

ROMULUS. We cannot possibly afford that, dear Julia. We have not paid for the chicken feed.

ZENO. Amazing. A world goes up in flames and you make silly jokes. Every day thousands of human beings are dying and here you muddle along. What does chicken feed have to do with the approach of the Barbarians?

ROMULUS. I have my worries, too, after all.

ZENO. It seems you have not recognized the full extent of the Teutonic threat to the world. (*He drums with his fingers on the table.*)

JULIA. That is exactly what I have been saying, over and over again.

ZENO. But the success of the Teutons cannot merely be explained on material grounds. We must look deeper than that. Our cities surrender, our soldiers defect, our peoples no longer believe in us because we doubt ourselves. We must pull ourselves together, Romulus, we must think of our ancient greatness, we must recall Caesar, Augustus, Trajan, and Constantine. There is no other way; without belief in ourselves and in our political mission, we are lost.

ROMULUS. All right then, let us believe.

(*Silence. Everyone sits in an attitude of devotion.*)

ZENO. You really believe? (*He seems somewhat unsure.*)

ROMULUS. Firm as a rock.

ZENO. In our ancient greatness?

ROMULUS. In our ancient greatness.

ZENO. In our historic mission?

ROMULUS. In our historic mission.

ZENO. And you, Empress Julia?

JULIA. My belief has always been firm.

(ZENO *feels easier.*)

ZENO. A marvellous feeling, is it not? One can positively feel the positive power charging these rooms. High time, too.

(*All three continue in an attitude of great belief.*)

ROMULUS. And now?

ZENO. What do you mean?

ROMULUS. Well, now that we believe?

ZENO. That is the main thing.

ROMULUS. But what is to happen now?

ZENO. Unimportant.

ROMULUS. But we must do something now that we think positively.

ZENO. Everything else will happen all by itself. All we have to do is find an idea to set against the slogan of the Teutons: 'For freedom and liberty.' I propose 'For slavery and God.'

ROMULUS. I don't know whether God is on our side. Information on that is rather vague.

ZENO. 'For order against anarchy.'

ROMULUS. No, not that. Personally, I'm more in favour of a practical slogan, a proposition that can be realized. For example: 'For better agriculture and bigger chickens.'

JULIA. Romulus!

(MARES *rushes in from the left. He is beside himself.*)

MARES. The Teutons are marching on Rome!

(ZENO *and* JULIA *jump frightened to their feet.*)

ZENO. When is the next boat for Alexandria?

ROMULUS. Tomorrow morning, half past eight. What do you want there?

ZENO. To plead for asylum with the Emperor of Abyssinia. Even from there I shall continue my indefatigable fight against the Teutonic menace. Though at times it seems to me it would be better to fall into the hands of the Teutons than into the clutches of my chamberlains.

(*The* EMPRESS *gathers composure.*)

JULIA. The Teutons are marching on Rome and you are still eating your breakfast.

(*The* EMPEROR *rises with dignity.*)

ROMULUS. A politician's prerogative. Mares, I appoint you Field-Marshal of the Empire.

MARES. I will save Rome, my Emperor! (*He falls upon his knees and swings his sword about.*)

ROMULUS. That is just what I needed! (*He sits down again.*)

MARES. Only one thing can save us: total mobilization. (*He rises determinedly.*)

ROMULUS. And what do these words mean?

MARES. I just thought of them. Total mobilization means the most absolute and complete employment of all the forces of a nation for military purposes.

ROMULUS. Purely stylistically, I do not like that.

MARES. Total mobilization must be established in all those parts of the empire not yet occupied by the enemy.

ZENO. The Field-Marshal is right. Only total mobilization can save us. That is the very idea we were looking for. 'Total mobilization' is something everyone will understand.

ROMULUS. Ever since men clubbed each other, war has been a crime; total mobilization will make it lunacy. I put the fifty members of my personal guard at your disposal, Marshal.

MARES. Your Majesty! Odoaker has an army of one hundred thousand Teutons, all well armed.

ROMULUS. The greater the general, the fewer troops he needs.

MARES. Never in history has a Roman general been so insulted.

(*He salutes and goes off to the left. In the meantime* APOLLONIUS *has taken down several busts, leaving only the one in the centre.*)

APOLLONIUS. Ten gold pieces for all that useless trash.

ROMULUS. I would prefer you to speak in more respectful tones of Rome's great past, Apollonius.

APOLLONIUS. The expression 'trash' refers only to your legacy's worth as antiques. It really does not represent an historic judgment.

ROMULUS. But you must give me the ten gold pieces immediately.

APOLLONIUS. Haven't I always, Your Majesty? I will leave one bust: that of King Romulus. (*He counts out ten gold pieces.*)

ROMULUS. But my namesake founded Rome!

APOLLONIUS. A beginner's effort. That is why it is already falling apart.

(*The* EMPEROR *of the Eastern Roman Empire is growing increasingly embarrassed.*)

ZENO. You failed to introduce me to this gentleman, Romulus.

ROMULUS. The Emperor of the Eastern Roman Empire, Zeno the Isaurian – Apollonius.

APOLLONIUS. Your Majesty. (*He bows coolly.*)

ZENO. You really should visit the Island of Patmos some time. It has remained loyal to me, my dear Apollonius, and there I own many unique pieces of Greek antiquity.

APOLLONIUS. Quite possibly I can arrange a visit some day, Your Majesty.

ZENO. Perhaps, then, since I shall be embarking for Alexandria tomorrow, you would grant me a small advance ...

APOLLONIUS. I am sorry. On principle I never pay imperial houses in advance. Times are too turbulent, and political institutions too unstable. And lately, the interest of my clients has turned from antiquity towards Teutonic handicraft. Primitive art is all the rage now. A horror, but de gustibus non est disputandum. May I take my leave of Your Majesties?

ROMULUS. I am sorry, Apollonius, that you were caught in the midst of the dissolution of my empire.

APOLLONIUS. I don't mind, Your Majesty. That is what I live off, as an antique dealer. I will send some of my porters for the busts I have lined up.

(*He bows once more and goes off to the left. The* EMPEROR *of the Eastern Empire shakes his head.*)

ZENO. I cannot understand it, Romulus. For years I have not been able to get any credit. Every day I see it more clearly: ours is not a profitable occupation.

(*The Minister of State,* TULLIUS ROTUNDUS, *enters from the left.*)

TULLIUS ROTUNDUS. Majesty!

ROMULUS. Is our athlete finally asleep, Tullius Rotundus?

TULLIUS ROTUNDUS. I didn't come to speak to you about Spurius Titus Mamma, but about Caesar Rupf.

ROMULUS. His name is unfamiliar.

TULLIUS ROTUNDUS. A very important person. He wrote Your Majesty a letter.

ROMULUS. Since I was inaugurated as emperor I haven't read letters. Who is he?

TULLIUS ROTUNDUS. A manufacturer of trousers. The producer of those Teutonic garments pulled up over one's legs. They are becoming quite the fashion with us.

ROMULUS. Is he rich?

TULLIUS ROTUNDUS. Incredibly rich.

ROMULUS. At last, a man who makes sense.

JULIA. You had best receive him immediately, Romulus.

ROMULUS. We await the manufacturer of trousers with pleasure.

(CAESAR RUPF *enters from the left. He is powerfully built, and dressed richly. He heads directly for* ZENO, *thinking him the Emperor, but* ZENO, *embarrassed, directs him towards* ROMULUS. CAESAR RUPF *holds a broad-rimmed travel hat of ancient design in his hand. He nods briefly.*)

CAESAR RUPF. Emperor Romulus.

ROMULUS. Welcome to you. This is my wife, the Empress Julia, and this, the Emperor of the Eastern Roman Empire, Zeno the Isaurian.

(CAESAR RUPF *nods very briefly.*)

ROMULUS. What do you wish of me, Caesar Rupf?

CAESAR RUPF. At the time of the Emperor Augustus, my forefathers came from Germania to settle in Rome. Ever since the first century, we have been the leaders of the garment industry.

ROMULUS. I am pleased to hear that. (*He hands* CAESAR'*s hat to a surprised* ZENO.)

CAESAR RUPF. When it comes to manufacturing trousers, Your Majesty, I go all out.

ROMULUS. Of course.

CAESAR RUPF. And I am, of course, also one hundred per cent aware that Rome's conservative circles are against trousers, just as they are against everything else that dawns new on the horizon.

ROMULUS. Where trousers commence, culture ends.

CAESAR RUPF. As Emperor you can, of course, afford this jest. But as a man of unclouded realism, I can quite soberly say: to trousers belongs the future. A modern state whose citizens do not wear trousers will go to pot. There is a profound inner connection between the fact that the Teutons wear trousers and that they are making such incredible progress. This inner connection may seem a Sphinxian puzzle to men who are first, last and always statesmen, but who never think in depth. For a man of business, however, it is as clear as daylight. Only a Rome that wears trousers will be equipped to meet the onslaught of the Germanic hordes.

ROMULUS. If I could share your optimism, my dear Caesar Rupf, I would don one of your fabled garments myself.

CAESAR RUPF. I have sworn, by all that is holy, to wear trousers only when it has dawned on the very simplest of souls that without trousers humanity might just as well crawl in a hole. Professional honour, Your Majesty, no compromising that. Either all men wear trousers or Caesar Rupf abdicates.

ROMULUS. And what do you propose?

CAESAR RUPF. Your Majesty, on one hand we have the international firm of Caesar Rupf and on the other, the Roman Empire. Correct?

ROMULUS. Certainly.

CAESAR RUPF. Let us call a diamond a diamond, not tarnished by any sentimentalities. Behind me stand a few million sesterces; behind you, the deluge.

ROMULUS. The difference cannot be put better.

CAESAR RUPF. First I thought I would buy up the whole Roman Empire.

(*The* EMPEROR *can hardly suppress his joyful excitement.*)

ROMULUS. Let us talk about this in all seriousness, Caesar Rupf. In any event, let me ennoble you. Achilles, a sword!

CAESAR RUPF. Thank you, Your Majesty, I have already bought myself every possible title. You see, to tell you the ice-cold truth, I decided against that deal. The Roman Empire is so run-down that to put it back on its feet would be too expensive, even for an international firm like mine. And no one could know if it would turn out to be a profitable deal. We might end up with a state colossus and that, too, would be no good. Either one is an international firm or an empire and I must say, quite frankly, an international firm is much more profitable. Therefore I decided against that purchase, Emperor Romulus, but I am not against an alliance.

ROMULUS. And just how do you imagine an alliance between the empire and your firm?

CAESAR RUPF. Organic, quite organic. As a businessman I am entirely for the organic. Think 'organic' or go broke, is my motto. First we have to put the Teutons out in the cold.

ROMULUS. Precisely that seems a little difficult.

CAESAR RUPF. A businessman of international stature does not know the word 'difficult', especially not when he commands the necessary pocket money. Odoaker, in answer to my direct inquiry, has declared himself ready to evacuate Italy for the sum of ten million.

ROMULUS. Odoaker?

CAESAR RUPF. The Teutonic Chief.

ROMULUS. Odd. Of all people I never thought he could be bought.

CAESAR RUPF. Every man has his price, Your Majesty.

ROMULUS. And what do you ask of me in return for this help?

CAESAR RUPF. I will pay the ten million and subsidize the empire with a few odd millions so that it might just keep its head above water like every other sound and healthy state, on one condition. One condition, I say, aside from the fact, of course, that trousers will be the obligatory dress; and that is, that you give me your daughter, Rea, for my wife. It is as clear as day that only in this way can the alliance be cemented organically.

ROMULUS. My daughter is engaged to an impoverished patrician who for three years has been languishing as a prisoner of the Teutons.

CAESAR RUPF. You see, Your Majesty, I am as cold as ice. You must admit, without batting an eye, that the Roman Empire can only be saved by an unshakeable alliance with an experienced business firm; otherwise the Teutons who lie in readiness before Rome will advance on us in leaps and bounds. This very afternoon you will give me your answer. If it is no, I will marry Odoaker's daughter. The firm of Rupf must have an heir. I am in the best years of my life and the storms and stresses of business life, compared to which your battles are mere child's play, have made it impossible for me till now to seek my happiness in the arms of a beloved spouse. It is not easy to choose between these two possibilities, although it would seem politically more natural to take the Teutonic princess without hesitation. However, my sense of gratitude towards my adopted homeland has swayed me to make this proposal to you. For I do not wish that the firm of Rupf should be suspected of partiality in the forum of history.

(He bows briefly, tears his hat out of ZENO*'s hand and goes off to the left. The other three remain sitting at the table. Stunned, they keep silent.)*

JULIA. Romulus, you must speak to Rea immediately.

ROMULUS. And what am I to say to our daughter, my dear wife?

JULIA. Simply that she will have to marry Caesar Rupf immediately.

ROMULUS. I will sell the Roman Empire for a handful of sesterces here and now, but I have not the faintest intention of bargaining away my daughter.

JULIA. Rea will voluntarily sacrifice herself for the empire.

ROMULUS. For centuries, we have sacrificed much to the state. Now it is time for the state to sacrifice itself for us.

JULIA. Romulus!

ZENO. If your daughter does not marry him now, the world will come to an end.

ROMULUS. We will come to an end. That's quite a difference.

ZENO. We are the world.

ROMULUS. We are provincials for whom the world has grown too large. We can no longer comprehend it.

ZENO. A man like you should not be Emperor of Rome. (*He beats his fist on the table and goes off to the right. Five pot-bellied porters enter from the left.*)

FIRST PORTER. We came to get the busts.

ROMULUS. Help yourselves, please. They are all lined up against the walls.

FIRST PORTER. Every one an emperor. Don't drop them. They are likely to crack.

(*The room is filled with porters who are carrying busts out.*)

JULIA. Romulus. They call me Julia, mother of our country. I am proud of this title. Let me speak to you now as the mother of my country. You sit the whole day over your breakfast. You are only interested in your chickens. You do not receive your courier. You refuse total mobilization. You do not advance against your enemy. You will not give your daughter to the one man who can save us. Just what *do* you want?

ROMULUS. I do not want to interfere with the course of history, my dear Julia.

JULIA. Then I'm ashamed to be your wife! (*She goes off to the right.*)

ROMULUS. You may clear the table, Pyramus. I have finished my morning repast. (*He wipes his mouth with a napkin.* PYRAMUS *carries the table out.*)

My finger bowl, Achilles.

(ACHILLES *brings a bowl filled with water.* ROMULUS *washes his hands.* SPURIUS TITUS MAMMA *rushes in from the left.*)

SPURIUS TITUS MAMMA. My Emperor. (*He falls upon his knee.*)

ROMULUS. Who are you?

SPURIUS TITUS MAMMA. Spurius Titus Mamma, Captain of Cavalry.

ROMULUS. What do you wish?

SPURIUS TITUS MAMMA. For two days and two nights, I rode here from Pavia. Seven horses collapsed under me. Three arrows wounded me and when I arrived they would not let me come to you. Here, my Emperor, is the final message from Orestes, your last general, before he fell into the enemy's hands. (*He hands a roll to the* EMPEROR. *The* EMPEROR *remains unmoved.*)

ROMULUS. You are exhausted and wounded. Why this extraordinary effort, Spurius Titus Mamma?

SPURIUS TITUS MAMMA. That Rome may live.

ROMULUS. Rome died long ago. You are sacrificing yourself for a corpse. You are fighting for a shadow. The country you live for is no more than a grave. Go to sleep, Captain, our times have turned your heroism into a pose.

(*He rises majestically and goes out through the door in the centre.* SPURIUS TITUS MAMMA *rises very disturbed, then suddenly throws the message of Orestes on the floor, stamps upon it, and screams.*)

SPURIUS TITUS MAMMA. Emperor, you're a disgrace to Rome!

ACT TWO

The afternoon of the fateful day in March in the year 476. A park, with the EMPEROR*'s villa in the rear. Chickens are clucking, cocks are crowing and now and again a fowl flies across the stage, especially whenever someone comes in. The porch of the dilapidated villa is covered with chicken dirt. A door opens on to the porch, and some steps lead from the porch into the park. On the walls of the villa is inscribed in chalk: 'Long Live Independence, Long Live Liberty!' The impression of the scene is that of a chicken yard, even though in the right foreground there are a few rather elegant garden chairs which have seen better days. From time to time thick dark smoke rises from a low building in the rear. The chancery lies slightly to the left of stage at right angles to the villa. The mood is one of enormous despair, of the sense of the decline of the world, 'après nous le déluge.'*

Characters: TULLIUS ROTUNDUS *sits on one chair; on another the Minister of War,* MARES, *now Rome's Marshal, sits asleep in full armour, a map of Italy spread across his knees, his helmet and baton lying next to him on the ground. His shield is leaning against the wall of the house. It, too, has the Teutonic slogan smeared upon it.* SPURIUS TITUS MAMMA, *who is still very dirty and bandaged, drags himself along the wall, leans against it, then drags himself on.*

SPURIUS TITUS MAMMA. I am tired, so tired, I am dead tired.
(*A cook dressed in a white apron and tall cook's hat appears in the door of the villa.*)

COOK. I have the honour to announce the menu for tonight's dinner. Tonight, on the Ides of March anno 476, the company shall dine on soup Julienne and three fine hens stuffed with roasted chestnuts à la Campania.

(*Clucking and enticing the chickens, he strides off on to the porch towards the rear. He holds a knife hidden behind him. The chickens scatter in front.*)

COOK. Julius, Nepos, Orestes, Romulus, chick, chick, chick ...

(ZENO *the Isaurian appears from the left. He stops to scrape his sandals on the ground.*)

ZENO. Now I have stepped on another egg! Isn't there anything here but chickens? My sandals are all sticky and yellow.

TULLIUS ROTUNDUS. Raising chickens is the Emperor's sole passion.

(*A courier runs into the palace from the right.*)

COURIER. The Teutons are in Rome! The Teutons are in Rome!

TULLIUS ROTUNDUS. More bad tidings. Nothing but bad news all day long.

ZENO. And all on account of this mania for chickens. Let us hope the Emperor is at least praying right now in the chapel for his people.

TULLIUS ROTUNDUS. The Emperor is sleeping.

ZENO. We're trying feverishly to save civilization and the Emperor is asleep – what's that smell?

TULLIUS ROTUNDUS. We are burning the Emperor's archives.

(ZENO *is thunderstruck.*)

ZENO. You – are – burning the archives! Why, for heaven's sake?

TULLIUS ROTUNDUS. These invaluable documents of the Roman art of government must under no circumstances fall into the hands of the Teutons. To take them to safety costs money – and we lack the financial means.

ZENO. And so you just burn the archives? With a smile on your lips as if you did not believe in the final triumph of right. Your whole western empire is beyond all help – it is rotten to the core. No spirit, no courage ...

(*The two chamberlains appear from the right.*)

CHAMBERLAINS. Your Majesty.

ZENO. My chamberlains have escaped from the chicken yard.

(*He is frightened to death. The two take him by the hand.*)

SULPHURIDES. Your Majesty, we must repeat our verses of lamentations. It is of the most urgent necessity.

PHOSPHORIDOS. If you please, Zeno the Isaurian.

ZENO. I plead for help, O Sun ...

SULPHURIDES. O Moon.

ZENO. O Moon in this universe of darkest night. Pleading mercy, I approach you. Be it the moon ...

PHOSPHORIDOS. The sun.

ZENO. The sun – ouch, another egg!

(*He scrapes the egg off his sandals. Then he is led off by his chamberlains.*)

SPURIUS TITUS MAMMA. I've had no sleep for a hundred hours, for a hundred hours.

(*Chickens cackle fearfully. The* COOK *appears on the right, then disappears into the villa. In each hand he holds a chicken and another one under his right arm. His apron is covered with blood.*)

COOK. Call these things chickens! And I'm supposed to serve things like this! Each one named after an emperor and yet all so skinny. What good is it to be named after an emperor if they're so skinny they'll hardly make a good soup? Fortunately, we'll stuff them with chestnuts. That way at least their lordships will have something to fill their stomachs, even if it's only good for dogs.

SPURIUS TITUS MAMMA. This eternal cackling is driving me crazy. I am so tired, so dog-tired. Riding all the way here at the gallop from Pavia, after such enormous loss of blood.

TULLIUS ROTUNDUS. Go and rest behind the villa, the cackling is not as loud there.

SPURIUS TITUS MAMMA. Tried that already. But the princess is having her drama lessons there, and next to the pond the Emperor of the Eastern Roman Empire is practising ...

MARES. Quiet! (*He goes back to sleep.*)

TULLIUS ROTUNDUS. You really should not speak in such a loud voice or the Imperial Marshal will wake up.

SPURIUS TITUS MAMMA. I'm so unspeakably tired. And then there is all this smoke, this stinking burning smoke!

TULLIUS ROTUNDUS. Why not at least sit down?

SPURIUS TITUS MAMMA. If I sit down I'll fall asleep.

TULLIUS ROTUNDUS. That would be the most natural thing for you to do, being so tired.

SPURIUS TITUS MAMMA. I don't want sleep, I want revenge.

(*The* IMPERIAL MARSHAL *rises in despair.*)

MARES. Who can think and plan with all this noise going on? Strategy is a matter of intuition. Before making the bloody incision it is necessary, as in surgery, to attain a certain inner composure. In the conduct of war nothing is worse than wanton noise-making at headquarters.

(*Angrily, he rolls up his map, takes his helmet, and starts towards the house. Picking up his shield he looks at it, startled.*)

Someone scribbled the enemy's slogan on my shield. Even the walls of the palace have been defaced.

TULLIUS ROTUNDUS. The maidservant from Helvetia.

MARES. That calls for a court martial.

TULLIUS ROTUNDUS. Now really, this is no time for such things, Marshal.

MARES. Sabotage.

TULLIUS ROTUNDUS. Lack of personnel. After all, somebody has to help the Lord High Steward pack.

MARES. But you can help. As Minister of State, what else do you have to do now?

TULLIUS ROTUNDUS. I have to prepare the legal basis upon which the Emperor's residence may be moved to Sicily.

MARES. I shall not be led astray by your defeatism. Our strategic position grows more favourable hour by hour. It improves from defeat to defeat. The farther the Teutons dare to advance into our peninsula, the farther they will find themselves down a blind alley. Then we shall be able to squash them with ease from our bases in Sicily and Corsica.

TULLIUS ROTUNDUS. First squash the Emperor.

MARES. We simply *cannot* lose. The Teutons have no fleet. That makes us unassailable in our islands.

TULLIUS ROTUNDUS. But we have no fleet either! So what good are the islands to us? The Teutons will sit unassailable in Italy.

MARES. Then we shall build a fleet.

SPURIUS TITUS MAMMA. Build one! The empire is bankrupt.

TULLIUS ROTUNDUS. We'll worry about that later. Right now the main problem is how to get to Sicily.

MARES. I shall order a three-masted schooner.

TULLIUS ROTUNDUS. A three-master! We cannot possibly afford one. They're as expensive as sin. Just try to find a galley.

MARES. Now I've been demoted to a shipping agent.

(*He ambles off into the villa.*)

TULLIUS ROTUNDUS. You see, now you've woken the Imperial Marshal.

SPURIUS TITUS MAMMA. I am so tired.

TULLIUS ROTUNDUS. I only hope we'll find a villa in Sicily we can afford to rent.

(*Fearful cackling. From the left appears the ragged figure of* EMILIAN. *He is gaunt and pale. He looks around.*)

EMILIAN. Is this the Emperor's villa in Campania?

(*The* MINISTER OF STATE *looks astonished at the ghostlike figure.*)

TULLIUS ROTUNDUS. Who are you?

EMILIAN. A ghost.

TULLIUS ROTUNDUS. And what do you want?

EMILIAN. The Emperor is father to us all. Isn't that true?

TULLIUS ROTUNDUS. To all patriots.

EMILIAN. I am a patriot. I came to visit the house of my father.

(*He looks around again.*) What a filthy chicken yard. What a dilapidated villa. Call this a chancery? Look at that weather-beaten Venus by the pond, the ivy everywhere, the moss, eggs hidden in the weeds – some of them have got under my feet already – and somewhere, I'm sure, the Emperor must lie snoring.

TULLIUS ROTUNDUS. Better take yourself off or I shall whistle for the guards. They're exercising on the lawn in the park.

EMILIAN. They're sleeping on the lawn in the park, hypnotized by the cackling of the chickens. No need to disturb their peaceful slumber.

(*The* EMPRESS *appears in the doorway.*)

JULIA. Ebius! Ebius! Has anyone seen the Lord High Steward, Ebi?

EMILIAN. The mother of her country.

TULLIUS ROTUNDUS. Isn't he helping with the packing, Your Majesty?

JULIA. Since this morning he cannot be found anywhere.

TULLIUS ROTUNDUS. Then he must have fled already.

JULIA. Typically Teuton.

(*The* EMPRESS *exits.*)

SPURIUS TITUS MAMMA. When you come right down to it, it is the Romans who are fleeing!

(*For a moment he has grown extremely angry, but then his anger collapses. However, in order not to fall asleep he walks back and forth desperately.* EMILIAN *sits down in the Marshal's seat.*)

EMILIAN. Are you Tullius Rotundus, Minister of State?

TULLIUS ROTUNDUS. Oh, do you know me?

EMILIAN. In the past you, Tullius Rotundus, and I often sat together. On many summer evenings.

TULLIUS ROTUNDUS. I don't remember at all.

EMILIAN. How should you? In the meantime an empire has fallen.

TULLIUS ROTUNDUS. Tell me at least, where do you come from?

EMILIAN. From the world of reality, straight to this farce of an imperial residence.

SPURIUS TITUS MAMMA. I am tired, simply dog-tired.

(*More cackling of chickens.* MARES *comes out of the villa.*)

MARES. I forgot my marshal's baton.

EMILIAN. Here it is, Sir.

(*He gives the baton to the general.* MARES *waddles back into the villa.*)

TULLIUS ROTUNDUS. I understand: you have come from the front. You are a brave man. You have spilled your heart's blood for your country. What can I do for you?

EMILIAN. What can you do against the Teutons?

TULLIUS ROTUNDUS. Nobody can do anything against them directly. Our resistance is calculated on a long-range basis. The mills of God grind slowly.

EMILIAN. Then you cannot do anything for me.

(*Several porters bearing trunks come out of the villa.*)

ONE OF THE PORTERS. Where are we to take the Empress's trunks?

TULLIUS ROTUNDUS. To Naples.

(*The porters carry the trunks away, one by one. They dilly-dally. During the remainder of the scene one or other of the porters reappears now and again.*)

TULLIUS ROTUNDUS. These are bitter times. A tragic epoch. But still such a highly organized legal system as the Roman Empire will survive even the worst crises. Our superior culture, our higher standard of living will win out against the Teutons.

SPURIUS TITUS MAMMA. I'm so incredibly tired.

EMILIAN. Tell me, do you love our poet, Horace? Do you write in our finest classical style?

TULLIUS ROTUNDUS. I am a jurist.

EMILIAN. Once I loved Horace, and wrote in the finest classical style.

TULLIUS ROTUNDUS. Are you a poet, then?

EMILIAN. I was a representative of the highest culture.

TULLIUS ROTUNDUS. Then write again, create anew! Spirit conquers brute matter.

EMILIAN. Where I just came from, the brutes conquered the spirit.

(*Renewed cackling; more chickens flying about. From the right along the villa appears* REA *with* PHYLAX, *an actor.*)

REA. Do you, citizens of my father's land,
See me now go upon my last journey
And see me look upon
The last light of the sun.
And then nevermore?

SPURIUS TITUS MAMMA. If I listen to classical poetry now I'll fall asleep on the spot!

(*He staggers off to the left.*)

PHYLAX. Continue, dear Princess, more forcefully, more dramatically!

REA. The god of death who silences all
Leads me alive
To the shores of hell. Not for me was
The marriage hymn. Nor does a bridegroom
Sing to me, no, not one song, for see
I am betrothed to Acheron.

PHYLAX. For see, I am betrothed to Acheron.

REA. For see, I am betrothed to Acheron.

PHYLAX. More tragically, Princess, more rhythmically. More of a cry from within, more soul, or no one will buy these immortal verses from you. One feels that you do not have any real conception of Acheron, the god of death. You talk as if he were something abstract. You have not experienced him within yourself. He has remained literary for you, not real. Sad, terribly sad. Listen once again: For see, I am betrothed to Acheron.

REA. For see, I am betrothed to Acheron.

PHYLAX. Woe, a fool ...

REA. Woe, a fool you make of me, O my father's land!
Why do you mock me
Though I have not yet perished,
And while I still see the light of day, and why
Do you force me
With your shameful law
Unwept by loved ones into this monstrous grave!
Not one of the living, not one of the dead.

PHYLAX. Not one of the living, not one of the dead. Where is the tragedy, Princess? Where the feeling of immeasurable grief? Once again now: Not one of the living ...

REA. Not one of the living, not one of the dead!

(EMILIAN *has risen and stands before the reciting* PRINCESS. *She stares at him in amazement.*)

What do you want?

EMILIAN. Who are you?

REA. I should think I have a better right to ask you who you are.

EMILIAN. I am what comes back when one has been where I have. Who are you?

REA. I am Rea, the Emperor's daughter.

EMILIAN. Rea, the Emperor's daughter? I did not recognize you. You are beautiful, but I had forgotten your face.

REA. Did we know each other?

EMILIAN. I believe – yes, I remember – we once did.

REA. Do you come from Ravenna? Did we play together as children?

EMILIAN. We played together when I was a man.

REA. Won't you tell me who you are?

EMILIAN. My name is written in my left hand.

(*He shows his left hand.*)

REA. Oh, how terrible!

EMILIAN. Shall I withdraw my hand?

REA. I cannot bear to look at it.

(*She turns away.*)

EMILIAN. Then you will never know who I am.
(*He hides his hand.*)

REA. Give me your hand! (*She offers her right hand.* EMILIAN *puts his left into hers.*) This ring! Emilian's ring!

EMILIAN. Your bridegroom's ring, yes.

REA. But he is dead.

EMILIAN. Croaked.

REA. The ring's partly embedded in the flesh.
(*She stares at the hand lying in hers.*)

EMILIAN. This branded flesh and ring are one.

REA. Emilian! You are Emilian!

EMILIAN. I was.

REA. I no longer recognize you, Emilian.
(*She stares at him again.*)

EMILIAN. You will never recognize me again. Though I've come back I've been prisoner of the Teutons.
(*They stand and stare at each other.*)

REA. I waited for you three years.

EMILIAN. In a Teutonic dungeon three years are an eternity, Daughter of the Emperor. No one should wait as long as that for anybody.

REA. But now you are here. Come, come with me into my father's house.

EMILIAN. The Teutons are coming.

REA. We know.

EMILIAN. Then go, get a knife.
(*The* PRINCESS *looks at him, frightened.*)

REA. What do you mean, Emilian?

EMILIAN. I mean, even a woman can fight with a knife.

REA. We must not fight any more. The Roman armies are beaten. We have no more soldiers.

EMILIAN. Soldiers are just human beings and any human being can fight. There are still many people here. Women, slaves, old folks, cripples, children, ministers. Go, get a knife.

REA. That makes no sense, Emilian. We must surrender to the Teutons.

EMILIAN. I had to surrender to the Teutons three years ago. Look at what they made of me, Daughter of the Emperor. Go, get a knife.

REA. I waited for you three years. Day after day, hour after hour. And now I am frightened of you.

EMILIAN. 'For see, I am betrothed to Acheron.' Did you not just recite those verses? They've turned into reality, your verses. Go, get a knife. Hurry! Hurry!

(REA *flees into the house.*)

PHYLAX. But Princess! Your lesson is not over yet. The climax is still to come. A particularly elevated passage about Hades. The most beautiful in all classical literature.

REA. I have no need of literature any more. Now I know what the god of death is like.

(*She disappears into the villa. The actor rushes after her.*)

TULLIUS ROTUNDUS. Marcus Junius Emilian, returned from Teutonic prison. I am profoundly moved.

EMILIAN. Then profoundly move up to the front. Else you are profoundly full of luxury.

TULLIUS ROTUNDUS. My dear friend, surely you suffered much and deserve our respect. But you must not just assume that *we* here at the Emperor's residence have not suffered as well. To sit here and receive sad tidings after sad tidings, without being able to do anything about it all, that, no doubt, is the worst that can happen to a man of politics.

(*A courier runs into the palace from the left.*)

COURIER. The Teutons are marching along the Via Appia towards the south. The Teutons are marching along the Via Appia towards the south.

TULLIUS ROTUNDUS. You see! Towards the south. Directly towards us. We hardly finished mentioning one bad tiding when a new one comes.

(MARES *appears in the door of the villa.*)

MARES. No galley to be had far and wide.

TULLIUS ROTUNDUS. But there is one anchored in the harbour at Naples.

MARES. It floated over to the Teutons.

TULLIUS ROTUNDUS. But for heaven's sake, Marshal, we *must* have a ship.

MARES. I'll try to get a fisherman's boat.

(*He disappears again. The* MINISTER OF STATE *is angry.*)

TULLIUS ROTUNDUS. You see, here I was all prepared to reorganize the Empire from Sicily. I have planned social reforms, right down to disability insurance for the dock workers. But, of course, I can only put these plans into effect if we find a vessel!

SPURIUS TITUS MAMMA. This smoke, this eternal acrid smoke.

(*Cackling of hens.* CAESAR RUPF *enters from the left.*)

CAESAR RUPF. Gentlemen, I hope it is crystal clear to you that after the fall of Rome the empire will not be worth a scrap of paper. Bankruptcy has been coupled with a military fiasco; the Roman Empire will never be able to pull itself out of this quagmire.

EMILIAN. Who are you?

CAESAR RUPF. Caesar Rupf, owner of the international firm of Rupf, coats and trousers.

EMILIAN. What do you want?

CAESAR RUPF. It must be as clear as daylight to even a partially informed politician that there is but one way to save Rome: that is, for me to put up a few millions. I demand that, for the honest offer I have made, I receive a decent answer. Yes or No. Wedding feast or world defeat. Either I return home with a bride or the Empire can go to the dogs.

EMILIAN. What's going on here, Minister of State?

TULLIUS ROTUNDUS. Odoaker agreed to evacuate Italy for the sum of ten million. This – manufacturer of trousers – is willing to pay that sum.

EMILIAN. His conditions?

TULLIUS ROTUNDUS. That Princess Rea marry him.

EMILIAN. Go, get the Princess.

TULLIUS ROTUNDUS. You mean ...

EMILIAN. And call the entire court together.

(*The* MINISTER OF STATE *goes into the villa.*)

EMILIAN. You shall have your answer, Sir.

(*The* CAPTAIN OF CAVALRY *staggers from the right to the left of the stage.*)

SPURIUS TITUS MAMMA. For a hundred hours I haven't slept. A hundred hours. I am so tired, so tired. I could drop dead.

(*In the door of the villa there appear* REA, TULLIUS ROTUNDUS, ZENO, MARES, PHOSPHORIDOS, SULPHURIDES, *the* COOK *and the guards.*)

REA. You called me, Emilian?

EMILIAN. Yes, I called you. Come to me.

(REA *slowly approaches* EMILIAN.)

EMILIAN. You waited three years for me, Daughter of the Emperor?

REA. Three years, day after day, night after night, hour after hour.

EMILIAN. You love me?

REA. I love you.

EMILIAN. With all your heart?

REA. With all my heart.

EMILIAN. And would do anything I ask you?

REA. I will do anything.

EMILIAN. Even take a knife?

REA. I will take a knife, if you wish it.

EMILIAN. So great is your love, Daughter of the Emperor?

REA. My love for you is beyond all measure. I no longer know you, but I love you. I am frightened of you, but I love you.

EMILIAN. Then marry this splendid pot-belly and bear him children.

(*He points to* CAESAR RUPF.)

ZENO. At last, a reasonable West Roman.

THE COURT. Marry, Princess, marry!

TULLIUS ROTUNDUS. Make this sacrifice for your country, my girl!

(*All stare at* REA, *full of hope.*)

REA. And leave you?

EMILIAN. You must leave me.

REA. And love another?

EMILIAN. Yes, love him who alone can save your country.

REA. But I love you.

EMILIAN. I cast you off so that Rome may live.

REA. You want to wound me as you have been wounded, Emilian.

EMILIAN. We must do what is necessary. Our shame will nourish Italy; our dishonour renew its strength.

REA. If you really loved me, you would not ask this of me.

EMILIAN. I can ask this of you only because you love me.

(*She looks at him in fright.*)

EMILIAN. You will obey, Daughter of the Emperor. Your love is beyond all measure.

REA. I will obey.

EMILIAN. You will be his wife?

REA. I shall be his wife.

EMILIAN. Then give your hand to this man, this trouser-manufacturer, who knows his own mind, clear and cold as ice. (REA *obeys.*)

Now, Caesar Rupf, the Emperor's only daughter has given you her hand. See, all of you, the golden bull is crowned with an imperial bridal wreath, for in our day, when mankind is being outraged as never before, coupling is a virtue.

(CAESAR RUPF *is deeply moved.*)

CAESAR RUPF. Princess, you must believe me, the tears in my eyes are as genuine as gold. By this union the international firm of Rupf has reached a pinnacle of success never before attained in my line.

(*Huge columns of smoke.*)

MARES. The empire is saved.

COOK. Western culture preserved! To celebrate this day I will roast Flavian.

SULPHURIDES AND PHOSPHORIDOS. Your Majesty, the Ode of Joy!

BOTH TOGETHER WITH ZENO.

O Byzantium, joy be thine!
Your name and fame like flames outshine
The moon and stars and sun.

Yea, our faith and hopes have been
Wondrously fulfilled again.
Salvation is ours, O Byzantium!

TULLIUS ROTUNDUS. Stop the burning of the archives this very instant.

VOICE OF ACHILLES. The Emperor!

(*The smoke clears away. The* EMPEROR, *surrounded by his Court, appears in the doorway.* ACHILLES *and* PYRAMUS *are behind him.* PYRAMUS *is carrying a flat basket. Silence.*)

ROMULUS. You are lively and in high spirits. What is the reason for all these goings-on?

(*Silence.*)

EMILIAN. Welcome, O Caesar of the good dinner-table. Greetings unto you, Emperor of fine fowl. Hail unto you whom your soldiers call Romulus the Little.

(*The* EMPEROR *looks attentively at* EMILIAN.)

ROMULUS. Hail unto you, Emilian, my daughter's bridegroom.

EMILIAN. You are the first to recognize me, Emperor Romulus. Not even your daughter knew me.

ROMULUS. Doubt not her love, though. Old age simply has sharper eyes. Emilian, be welcomed.

EMILIAN. Forgive me, Father of the world, for not responding perhaps to your greeting as is customary. For too long I was a prisoner of the Teutons. Now I no longer know the customs of your court. But knowing Rome's history will help me. There were emperors who were hailed thus: Well won, O mighty one. And others: Well murdered, Your Majesty, and thus you shall be hailed: Well slept, Emperor Romulus.

(*The* EMPEROR *sits down on an easy chair in the doorway and looks for a long time at* EMILIAN.)

ROMULUS. Your body bears witness to great want and tribulation. You suffered hunger and thirst.

EMILIAN. I went hungry and you ate your meals.

ROMULUS. I see your hands. You were tortured.

EMILIAN. I was tortured while your chickens flourished.

ROMULUS. You are full of despair.

EMILIAN. I escaped from my prison in Germania. I came to you on foot, Emperor of Rome. I measured the vast expanse of your dominions, mile after mile, step after step. I saw your empire, Father of the world ...

ROMULUS. Since I've been Emperor I have not left my country residence. Tell me about my empire, Emilian.

EMILIAN. Wherever I went I saw nothing but immense decay.

ROMULUS. Tell me of my subjects.

EMILIAN. Your people have been robbed by war profiteers, cheated by black marketeers, oppressed by mercenaries, jeered at by Teutonic soldiers.

ROMULUS. I'm not ignorant of these things.

EMILIAN. How can you know what you have never seen, Emperor of Rome?

ROMULUS. I can imagine it, Emilian. Come into my house. My daughter has been waiting for you these many years.

EMILIAN. I'm no longer worthy of your daughter, Emperor of Rome.

ROMULUS. You are not unworthy – only unhappy.

EMILIAN. I've been dishonoured. The Teutons forced me to crawl beneath a blood-smeared yoke. Naked. Like a beast.

MARES. Revenge!

REA. Emilian!

(*She embraces her betrothed.*)

EMILIAN. I'm a Roman officer. I've lost my honour. Go to him, Daughter of the Emperor, go to the man you now belong to.

(REA *steps slowly back to* CAESAR RUPF.)

EMILIAN. Your daughter has become the wife of this trouser-manufacturer, Emperor of Rome, and my shame has saved the empire.

(*The* EMPEROR *rises.*)

ROMULUS. The Emperor will not permit this marriage.

(*All stand as if turned to stone.*)

CAESAR RUPF. Papa!

REA. I shall marry him, Father. You cannot keep me from doing the one thing that will save my country.

ROMULUS. My daughter will submit to the Emperor's will. The Emperor knows what he is doing when he throws his empire to the flames, when he lets fall what must break, when he grinds under foot what is doomed.

(REA, *head bowed, goes into the house.*)

ROMULUS. To our duties, Pyramus. The chicken feed! Augustus! Tiberius! Trajan! Hadrian! Marcus Aurelius! Odoaker!

(*He goes off to the right, scattering chicken feed. His chamberlains follow him. The rest of the Court stand without moving.*)

TULLIUS ROTUNDUS. Better start burning the archives again!

(*Everything is again enveloped in heavy smoke.*)

EMILIAN. Down with the Emperor!

ACT THREE

The night of the Ides of March in the year 476 ... The Emperor's bedroom with a row of windows at left and a door at the back. On the right is a bed and another door. In the centre of the room stand two couches forming an angle that opens towards the audience. Between the couches stands a small, low, elegant table. In the foreground, both on the right and left, are two wardrobes. Near midnight. Full moon. The room lies in darkness except for the light which falls through the windows on to the floor and walls. The door at the back opens. PYRAMUS *appears with a three-armed candelabra and with it lights a second candelabra standing by the bed. Then he places the candelabra he carries on the low table. The* EMPEROR *enters by the door on the right, dressed in a rather shabby nightshirt. Behind him* ACHILLES.

ROMULUS. My bath tonight did me doubly good: first, because we had a fine supper, and then after such a depressing day nothing helps as much as a good bath. Such days are not for me. I am an untragic human being, Achilles.

ACHILLES. Docs Your Majcsty wish to don the Emperor's toga or his dressing-gown?

ROMULUS. My dressing-gown. I shall not govern any more today.

ACHILLES. Your Majesty is supposed to sign the proclamation to the Roman people tonight.

ROMULUS. Tomorrow will do.

(ACHILLES *wants to help him put on the dressing-gown. The* EMPEROR *stops him.*)

ROMULUS. Bring me my imperial dressing-gown, Achilles. This one's too shabby.

ACHILLES. The Empress has already packed the imperial dressing-gown. It belonged to her father.

ROMULUS. Indeed. Well then, help me put on this rag.

(*He slips on the gown and takes the wreath off his head.*)

ROMULUS. What? The wreath was on my head all this time? I even forgot to take it off for my bath. Hang it up by my bed, Pyramus.

(*He gives the wreath to* PYRAMUS, *who hangs it up by the bed.*)

ROMULUS. How many leaves are left?

PYRAMUS. Two.

ROMULUS. My expenses today were enormous. (*The* EMPEROR *sighs and goes to the window.*) At last some fresh air. The wind has turned and blown the smoke away. This afternoon was a torture. But at least the archives are ashes. The only sensible order my Minister of State ever gave.

PYRAMUS. Future historians will bemoan this loss, O my Emperor.

ROMULUS. Nonsense. They will invent better sources than our imperial archives.

(*He sits down on the couch on the left.*)

ROMULUS. Hand me Catullus, Pyramus, or has my wife packed that scroll, too, since it belonged to her father's library?

PYRAMUS. It was packed, my Emperor.

ROMULUS. So be it. Then I shall just have to try to remember as much of Catullus as I can. Good verses are never wholly forgotten. A cup of wine, Achilles.

ACHILLES. Does Your Majesty wish to drink wine from Falerone or from Syracuse?

ROMULUS. From Falerone. In days like these one should drink the best.

(ACHILLES *places a large cup in front of the* EMPEROR. PYRAMUS *fills it.*)

PYRAMUS. This bottle of Falerone, vintage year 70, is all that's left, my Emperor.

ROMULUS. Then leave it here.

ACHILLES. The Empress, mother of our country, wishes to speak to Your Majesty.

ROMULUS. The Empress may enter. I shall not need this second candelabra.

(The chamberlains bow and leave. PYRAMUS *takes the candelabra standing nearest the bed. The foreground only is now lit. The background is bathed by the growing light of the moon.* JULIA *appears in the back.)*

JULIA. The Lord High Steward has gone over to the Teutons. I always warned you about Ebi.

ROMULUS. Well, should he as a Teuton die for us Romans?

(Silence.)

JULIA. I came to speak with you for the last time.

ROMULUS. You're wearing your travelling clothes, my dear wife.

JULIA. I'm leaving for Sicily tonight.

ROMULUS. Is the fishing boat ready?

JULIA. A raft.

ROMULUS. But isn't that a little dangerous?

JULIA. Staying is more dangerous.

(Silence.)

ROMULUS. I wish you a safe journey.

JULIA. Perhaps we shall not see each other for a long time.

ROMULUS. We shall never see each other again.

JULIA. I am determined to continue the resistance against the enemy from Sicily. At any price.

ROMULUS. Resistance at any price is the greatest nonsense there is.

JULIA. You are a defeatist.

ROMULUS. I only weigh the odds. If we defend ourselves, our fall will be bloodier. That may look grandiose, but what is the sense? Why burn a world already lost?

(Silence.)

JULIA. Then you really don't want Rea to marry this Caesar Rupf?

ROMULUS. No.

JULIA. And you don't wish to go to Sicily?

ROMULUS. The Emperor will not flee.

JULIA. That will cost you your head.

ROMULUS. Quite likely. But should that make me act headless now?

(*Silence.*)

JULIA. We've been married twenty years, Romulus.

ROMULUS. What do you wish to say to me when you remind me of this enormous fact?

JULIA. We once loved each other.

ROMULUS. You know you are lying.

(*Silence.*)

JULIA. Then you only married me in order to become Emperor.

ROMULUS. Precisely.

JULIA. You dare to say this calmly to my face?

ROMULUS. Of course. Our marriage was horrible, but I never committed the crime of keeping you in doubt for a single day why I had married you. I married you in order to become Emperor and you married me to become Empress. You became my wife because I was a descendant of the highest Roman nobility. And you were the daughter of the Emperor Valentian and a slave girl. I made you legitimate and you crowned me.

(*Silence.*)

JULIA. We needed each other.

ROMULUS. Precisely.

JULIA. Then it's your duty now to come with me to Sicily. We belong together.

ROMULUS. I have no more duties towards you. I gave you what you wanted from me. You became Empress.

JULIA. You cannot reproach me for anything. We acted the same way.

ROMULUS. No, we did not act the same way. Between your action and mine is an infinite difference.

JULIA. I cannot see that.

ROMULUS. You married me out of ambition. Everything you have ever done was done out of ambition. Even now, out of ambition, you will not give up this lost war.

JULIA. I'm going to Sicily because I love my country.

ROMULUS. You don't know your country. What you love is the abstract idea of a state which offered you the opportunity of becoming Empress by marriage.

(*The two are again silent.*)

JULIA. All right then, why not speak the truth? Why not be open with one another? I *am* ambitious. For me, there is nothing but the empire. I am the great-granddaughter of Julian, the last great Emperor. And proud of it. And what are you? The son of a bankrupt patrician. But you're ambitious, too, or you would not have become the Emperor of an entire world – you would have remained the nobody you were.

ROMULUS. What I did was dictated not by ambition but by necessity. What was the end for you was for me a means to an end. I became Emperor purely out of political insight.

JULIA. Political insight? When did you ever have any? In the twenty years of your reign you did nothing but eat, drink, sleep, read, and raise chickens. You never left your country estate, never entered your capital, and the financial reserves of the empire were so totally used up that now we must live like common labourers. Your only skill was to defeat with a joke any thought aimed at getting rid of you. But that your attitude is based on political insight is an enormous lie. Nero's megalomania and Caligula's madness were evidence of greater political maturity than your passion for chickens. Yours was no political insight but just plain indolence!

ROMULUS. Precisely. It was my political insight to do nothing.

JULIA. For that you didn't have to become Emperor.

ROMULUS. But that was the only way in which my doing nothing could make sense. To do nothing as a private citizen is completely ineffectual.

JULIA. And to do nothing as Emperor jeopardizes the state.

ROMULUS. Precisely.

JULIA. What do you mean?

ROMULUS. You've discovered the meaning of my doing nothing.

JULIA. But you cannot possibly doubt the necessity of the state.

ROMULUS. I don't doubt the necessity of the state. I merely doubt the necessity of our state. Our state has become a world empire, an institution officially engaged in murder, plunder, suppression, and oppressive taxation at the expense of other people – until I came along.

JULIA. Then I don't understand why, of all things, you had to become Emperor if that is what you thought about the Roman Empire.

ROMULUS. For hundreds of years now the Roman Empire has existed only because there was still an Emperor. Therefore, only by becoming Emperor did I have the opportunity to liquidate the empire.

JULIA. Either you are mad or the world is.

ROMULUS. I think the latter.

JULIA. Then you only married me in order to destroy the empire.

ROMULUS. For no other reason.

JULIA. And from the very beginning you planned for nothing but Rome's fall.

ROMULUS. For nothing else.

JULIA. Then you deliberately sabotaged any attempts to save the Empire?

ROMULUS. Deliberately.

JULIA. You acted the cynic and the perpetual over-stuffed buffoon in order to stab us in the back?

ROMULUS. You can put it that way if you like.

JULIA. You deceived me.

ROMULUS. You deceived yourself about me. You thought I was just as power-mad as you. You had it all figured out, but your calculation was wrong.

JULIA. Your calculation is coming out all right.

ROMULUS. Rome is falling.

JULIA. You are Rome's traitor.

ROMULUS. No, Rome's judge.

(*They are silent. Then* JULIA *cries out in despair.*)

JULIA. Romulus!

ROMULUS. You had better leave for Sicily now. I have nothing more to say to you.

(*Slowly the* EMPRESS *leaves.* ACHILLES *steps out of the background.*)

ACHILLES. My Emperor.

ROMULUS. My cup is empty. Fill it again.

(ACHILLES *fills the cup.*)

ROMULUS. You are trembling.

ACHILLES. Indeed, my Emperor.

ROMULUS. What is the matter with you?

ACHILLES. Your Majesty doesn't like me to discuss the military situation.

ROMULUS. You know that I expressly forbade you to do so. I only talk about the military situation with my barber. He is the only one who understands something about it.

ACHILLES. But Capua has fallen.

ROMULUS. That is no excuse whatever to spill good wine.

ACHILLES. I beg your pardon.

(*He bows.*)

ROMULUS. Now go to sleep.

ACHILLES. The Princess would like to speak to Your Majesty.

ROMULUS. My daughter may enter.

(ACHILLES *leaves.* REA *comes from behind.*)

REA. Father.

ROMULUS. Come, come, sit down by me.

(REA *sits down by him.*)

ROMULUS. What do you wish to tell me?

REA. Rome is in danger, Father.

ROMULUS. It is odd that tonight of all nights everyone wants to discuss politics with me. The noon meal is really the proper time for that.

REA. What shall I talk about then?

ROMULUS. About things one talks to one's father about at night. About things closest to your heart, my child.

REA. Rome is closest to my heart.

ROMULUS. Then you no longer love Emilian for whom you waited so long?

REA. But I do, Father.

ROMULUS. But no longer as passionately as before, no longer the way you once loved him?

REA. I love him more than my own life.

ROMULUS. Then talk to me about Emilian. If you love him, then he is more important than our run-down empire.

(*Silence.*)

REA. Father, let me marry Caesar Rupf.

ROMULUS. My dear daughter, I find this Rupf fellow quite congenial because he has money, but his conditions are unacceptable.

REA. He will save Rome.

ROMULUS. Precisely. This is what makes this man so unnatural. A garment manufacturer who wants to save the Roman Empire must be mad.

REA. There's no other way to save our country.

ROMULUS. I admit there is no other way. The country can only be saved with money, or it will surely be lost. But we must choose between a catastrophic capitalism and a capital catastrophe. So my dear child, you simply cannot marry this Caesar Rupf; you love Emilian.

(*Silence.*)

REA. I must leave him to serve my country.

ROMULUS. That is easily said.

REA. My country, above all.

ROMULUS. You see, you studied tragedy too much.

REA. But shouldn't one love one's country more than anything else in the world?

ROMULUS. No, one should never love it as much as one loves other human beings. Above all, always keep an open mind about any country. A country turns killer more easily than any man.

REA. Father.

ROMULUS. Yes, Daughter.

REA. I cannot possibly let my country down.

ROMULUS. You must.

REA. I cannot live without a country.

ROMULUS. Can you live without your beloved? To remain loyal to a human being is greater and much more difficult than to remain loyal to a state.

REA. It is my country, not just a state.

ROMULUS. Every state calls itself 'country', or 'nation', when it is about to commit murder.

REA. Our unconditional love for our country was what made Rome great.

ROMULUS. But our love did not make Rome good. With our virtues we nurtured a beast. We became drunk on the greatness of our country as on wine, but now what we love has turned into gall and wormwood.

REA. You are ungrateful to your country.

ROMULUS. No. Only I am not like that sire of heroes in one of your tragedies who says 'good appetite' to the state when the state wants to devour one of his children. Go, marry Emilian!

REA. Emilian has rejected me, Father.

ROMULUS. If there remains one spark of love in your body, you will not let this separate you from your lover. You will remain with him even when he rejects you. You will stick by him even if he is a criminal. But you can be separated from your country. Shake its dust off your feet when it has become a murderer's den and a place of execution, for then your love for your country is powerless.

(*Silence. A human figure climbs through the window on the left and then hides somewhere in the dark at the back.*)

REA. If I go back to him now he will surely reject me again. He will always reject me.

ROMULUS. Then you must simply keep on going back to him.

REA. He no longer loves me. He loves only Rome.

ROMULUS. Rome will come to an end and then all he will have left is your love.

REA. I am afraid.

ROMULUS. Learn to conquer your fears. That is the only art we must learn to master these days. Learn to look at things fearlessly and fearlessly to do the right thing. I've been trying to practise this all my life. Now, you try it, too. Go to him.

REA. Yes, Father, I will.

ROMULUS. Well said, my child. This is how I love you. Go to Emilian. Take leave of me. You will never see me again, for I shall die.

REA. Father!

ROMULUS. The Teutons will kill me. I have always counted on that death. That is my secret. I sacrifice Rome through sacrificing myself.

(*Silence.*)

REA. My Father.

ROMULUS. But you will live. Now go, my child; go to Emilian.

(REA *slowly leaves.* PYRAMUS *steps out of the background.*)

PYRAMUS. My Emperor.

ROMULUS. What do you wish?

PYRAMUS. The Empress has left.

ROMULUS. That is well.

PYRAMUS. Does Your Majesty wish to go to bed?

ROMULUS. Not yet. First I must have a talk with one other person. Bring me a second cup.

PYRAMUS. Yes, my Emperor.

(*He brings a second cup.*)

ROMULUS. Here, put it next to mine and fill it.

(PYRAMUS *fills it.*)

ROMULUS. And now mine, too.

(PYRAMUS *fills the* EMPEROR'*s cup.*)

PYRAMUS. The bottle is empty, my Emperor.

ROMULUS. Then you may go to sleep.

(PYRAMUS *bows and exits.* ROMULUS *sits without moving till the chamberlain's steps are no longer heard.*)

ROMULUS. Emilian, come forward. We are alone now.

(EMILIAN *slowly comes out of the darkness, wrapped in a black cloak.*)

EMILIAN. You knew I was here?

ROMULUS. A few seconds ago you climbed into my room through the window. My wine cup reflected your figure. Sit down.

EMILIAN. I shall stand.

ROMULUS. You came very late. It is midnight.

EMILIAN. Some visits are made only at midnight.

ROMULUS. You see, I was ready to receive you. To welcome you I had this cup filled with excellent wine. Let us touch glasses.

EMILIAN. So be it.

ROMULUS. To your homecoming.

EMILIAN. To that which shall be fulfilled this midnight.

ROMULUS. And what is that?

EMILIAN. Let us toast justice, Emperor Romulus.

ROMULUS. Justice is a terrible thing, Emilian.

EMILIAN. Terrible, like my wounds.

ROMULUS. All right then: To justice.

EMILIAN. We are alone. Only the darkness is witness to this moment when the Emperor of Rome and a man just returned from his Teutonic prison toast justice with cups of blood-red wine.

(ROMULUS *rises and they touch glasses. At the same instant someone cries out and from under the couch of the Emperor the head of* TULLIUS ROTUNDUS *appears.*)

ROMULUS. For heaven's sake, my dear Minister, has something happened to you?

TULLIUS ROTUNDUS. Your Majesty stepped on my fingers.

(He moans.)

ROMULUS. I'm sorry, but I couldn't possibly know you were under there. Every Minister of State cries out when justice is toasted.

TULLIUS ROTUNDUS. I merely wanted to propose to Your Majesty an all-inclusive old age insurance programme for the Roman Empire.

(He crawls out from under the bed, not without some embarrassment, dressed in a black cloak similar to EMILIAN'S.*)*

ROMULUS. Your hand is bleeding, Tullius Rotundus.

TULLIUS ROTUNDUS. From fright I scratched myself with my dagger.

ROMULUS. My dear Tullius, one must be very careful with daggers.

(He walks towards the left.)

EMILIAN. Are you going to call your chamberlains, Emperor Romulus?

(They face one another, EMILIAN *hostile and resolute,* ROMULUS *smiling.)*

ROMULUS. What for, Emilian? You know perfectly well they are asleep by midnight. But I do want to get a bandage for my wounded Minister of State.

(He goes to the wardrobe on the left and opens it. Inside the wardrobe stands, somewhat bent, ZENO *the Isaurian.)*

ROMULUS. Forgive me, Emperor of East Rome. I didn't know you were sleeping in my wardrobe.

ZENO. Oh, you are excused. Ever since I fled from Constantinople my insecure life has accustomed me to this sort of thing.

ROMULUS. I'm sincerely sorry you have such troubles.

*(*ZENO *climbs out of the wardrobe. He, too, is dressed in a black cloak. He looks about astonished.)*

ZENO. Why, is someone else here?

ROMULUS. Don't be disturbed. They came in quite by chance.

(*He takes a cloth from an upper shelf of the wardrobe.*)

ROMULUS. Amazing! There is yet another person in here.

ZENO. My chamberlain, Sulphurides.

(SULPHURIDES *climbs out. He is extremely tall. He is also dressed in a black cloak. He bows ceremoniously before* ROMULUS. ROMULUS *looks at him.*)

ROMULUS. Good evening. You should really have placed him in the other wardrobe, my Imperial Brother. And where did you put your chamberlain Phosphoridos?

ZENO. He's still under your bed, Emperor Romulus.

ROMULUS. He might as well come out, too. He need not be embarrassed.

(PHOSPHORIDOS, *who is a short man, crawls out from under the Emperor's bed. He, too, is dressed in a black cloak.*)

SULPHURIDES. We have come, Your Majesty ...

PHOSPHORIDES. To recite our ode of woe.

SULPHURIDES. The complete recital of which Your Majesty has not yet had the pleasure to hear.

ROMULUS. By all means, only not at this silent midnight hour.

(ROMULUS *sits down and gives the cloth to* TULLIUS ROTUNDUS.)

ROMULUS. Bind your wounds with this cloth, my dear Minister. I don't like to see blood.

(*The door of the wardrobe on the right falls open and* SPURIUS TITUS MAMMA *falls full length to the floor with a crash.*)

ROMULUS. Well, even our athlete is not asleep yet?

SPURIUS TITUS MAMMA. I am tired, simply dead tired.

(*He gets up unsteadily.*)

ROMULUS. You lost your dagger, Spurius Titus Mamma.

(SPURIUS TITUS MAMMA, *with a frown, picks up his dagger, and hastily hides it under his cloak.*)

SPURIUS TITUS MAMMA. I haven't slept for one hundred and ten hours.

ROMULUS. Let anyone else present come forward.

(*From under the couch on the left crawls* MARES, *followed by a soldier. Both are wrapped in black cloaks.*)

MARES. Excuse me, my Emperor. I want to discuss the total mobilization.

ROMULUS. And whom did you bring along for this discussion, Marshal?

MARES. My adjutant.

(*The* COOK *with his tall white hat now crawls forth slowly from under the Emperor's couch. He, too, is wrapped in a black cloak. For the first time the* EMPEROR *is visibly moved.*)

ROMULUS. You, too, Cook? And with the very kitchen knife with which you slaughtered so many emperors?

(*With downcast eyes the* COOK *steps into the half-circle of men around the* EMPEROR.)

ROMULUS. I see you all dressed in black. You crawled forth from under my bed and my couch, and out of my wardrobes, after spending half the night there in very complicated and uncomfortable positions. Why?

(*Deep silence.*)

TULLIUS ROTUNDUS. We want to speak with you, Emperor Romulus.

ROMULUS. The Emperor was not aware that court ceremonial prescribes gymnastics for those wishing to speak with him.

(*He gets up and rings a bell.*)

ROMULUS. Pyramus! Achilles!

(ACHILLES *and* PYRAMUS, *dressed in their nightshirts and caps, rush forth trembling.*)

ACHILLES. My Emperor!

PYRAMUS. Majesty!

ROMULUS. My imperial toga, Achilles! My imperial wreath, Pyramus!

(ACHILLES *places the toga about the* EMPEROR'*s shoulders, and* PYRAMUS *the wreath upon his head.*)

ROMULUS. Take the table and cups out, Achilles. This is a solemn moment.

(ACHILLES *and* PYRAMUS *carry the table off to the right.*)

ROMULUS. Now, go back to sleep.

(PYRAMUS *and* ACHILLES *bow and leave, greatly confused and frightened.*)

ROMULUS. The Emperor is ready to hear all of you. What is it you have to say to him?

TULLIUS ROTUNDUS. We demand the provinces back.

MARES. Your legions.

EMILIAN. The Empire.

(*Deep silence.*)

ROMULUS. The Emperor doesn't owe you an accounting.

EMILIAN. You owe Rome an accounting.

ZENO. You must answer before history.

MARES. You depended on our power.

ROMULUS. I did not depend on your power. Had I acquired the world with your help, you would be justified. But I lost a world you never won. I passed it on out of my hands like a bad coin. I am free, I have nothing to do with you. You are but moths dancing about my light, shadows which will fade when I no longer shine.

(*The conspirators inch away from him towards the wall.*)

I owe an accounting to only *one* of you and to this one I shall now speak. Come forward, Emilian.

(EMILIAN *slowly steps forward from the right.*)

I cannot speak to you as to an officer who has lost his honour. I am a civilian and never understood what is meant by an officer's honour. But I will speak to you as to a human being who was tortured and who suffered greatly. I love you like a son, Emilian. For me you represent the final great argument against those who, like myself, refuse to defend themselves; in you I'm willing to see the militant challenge of the people, violated again and again, the victims of power defiled a thousand times. What do you demand of your Emperor, Emilian?

EMILIAN. I demand an answer, Emperor Romulus.

ROMULUS. You shall have your answer.

EMILIAN. What did you do to keep your people from falling into the hands of the Teutons?

ROMULUS. Nothing.

EMILIAN. What have you done to keep Rome from being violated as I was?

ROMULUS. Nothing.

EMILIAN. And how will you justify yourself? You are accused of having betrayed your empire.

ROMULUS. I didn't betray my empire; Rome betrayed herself. Rome knew the truth but chose violence. Rome knew humaneness but chose tyranny. Rome doubly demeaned herself: before her own people and before the other nations in her power. You are standing before an invisible throne, Emilian; before the throne of all the Roman Emperors, of whom I am the last. Shall I touch your eyes that you may see this throne, this pyramid of skulls down whose steps cascade rivers of blood in endless waterfalls, generating Rome's power? What kind of an answer do you expect I can hand down to you, as I sit on top of the colossus that is Roman history? What can be said about your wounds by your Emperor who sits enthroned above the corpses of his own sons and the sons of strangers, above the mound of human sacrifices swept to his feet by the wars of Rome's glory and the gladiatorial games for Rome's amusement? Rome has grown weak, a tottering old hag, but her guilt has not been expiated and her crimes not erased. Over night the new day has dawned. The curses of Rome's victims are being fulfilled. The axe is put to the trunk, the rotten tree is being felled. The Teutons are coming; we have spilled the stranger's blood; we must now pay back with our own. Don't turn away, Emilian, don't retreat before the majesty that is mine, rising before you, covered as it is with the ancient guilt of our history, making it more horrible than your own body. Now we are speaking of justice, the justice to which we drank. Answer my question now: Do we still have the right to defend ourselves? Do we still have the right to be more than victims?

(EMILIAN *is silent.*)

You are silent.

(EMILIAN *slowly retreats to those surrounding the* EMPEROR *in a wide half-circle.*)

You are stepping back among those who came to me like thieves in the night. Let us be honest with one another. Let there be not one hair's breadth of a lie, not one hand's width of deceit between us. I know what all of you are hiding under your black cloaks, I know what your hands are clutching. But you made one mistake. You thought you were coming to a man who could not defend himself, while I now spring upon you with the claws of truth and grip you with the teeth of justice. You aren't attacking me, but I'm attacking you. You aren't accusing me, but I'm accusing you. Defend yourselves! Don't you know before whom you stand? In full knowledge I brought about the fall of the country you wish to defend. I broke the ice on which you stepped and burned the foundation on which you built. Why do you cling so silently to the walls of my chamber? You have only one answer. Kill me if you believe I am in the wrong! But if in truth we no longer have a *right* to defend ourselves, then surrender to the Teutons. Answer me.

(*They remain silent.*)

Answer!

(EMILIAN *lifts his dagger on high.*)

EMILIAN (*shouts*). Long live Rome!

(*All draw their daggers and step towards* ROMULUS *who remains calmly seated. The daggers close in over him. At that moment a horrifying cry of fright can be heard at the back:* 'The Teutons are coming!' *Gripped by panic everyone rushes away through windows and doors. The* EMPEROR *does not move. Pale from fright,* PYRAMUS *and* ACHILLES *step out of the background.*)

ROMULUS. Well, where are they, the Teutons?

PYRAMUS. In Nola, Your Majesty.

ROMULUS. What is all the shouting about, then? Why, they cannot be here before tomorrow morning. I shall go to bed now.

(*He rises.*)

PYRAMUS. Very well, my Emperor.

(PYRAMUS *takes off the* EMPEROR'*s toga, his wreath, and his robe.* ROMULUS, *going to his bed, suddenly stops.*)

ROMULUS. I see one of them still lying here in front of my bed, Achilles. Who is it?

(*The chamberlain lights up the body with a candelabra.*)

ACHILLES. It is Spurius Titus Mamma, Your Majesty, sound asleep.

ROMULUS. Heavens be thanked. Our athlete is asleep at last. Let him lie.

(ROMULUS *steps over him into his bed.* PYRAMUS *blows out the candles and goes off with* ACHILLES *in the dark.*)

ROMULUS. Pyramus!

PYRAMUS. Yes, my Emperor.

ROMULUS. When the Teutons arrive, let them come in.

ACT FOUR

The morning following the Ides of March in the year 476.

The Emperor's study as in ACT ONE. *Now only the bust of the founder of Rome, King Romulus, sits over the door at the back.* ACHILLES *and* PYRAMUS, *awaiting the* EMPEROR, *are standing by the door.)*

ACHILLES. A beautiful morning, a refreshing morning.

PYRAMUS. I cannot understand it: even on this day when the world's coming to an end the sun still rises.

ACHILLES. There's no depending even on nature.

(*Silence.*)

PYRAMUS. For sixty years, under eleven emperors, we have served Rome. To me it is historically incomprehensible that Rome should cease to exist during our lifetime.

ACHILLES. I'm washing my hands in innocence. I was always a perfect chamberlain.

PYRAMUS. Indeed. In every respect, we were the only really solid pillars of the empire.

ACHILLES. With our office, antiquity will end.

(*Silence.*)

PYRAMUS. To think the day is coming when neither Latin nor Greek will be spoken, only an impossible tongue like Teutonic.

ACHILLES. Imagine men at the helm of world politics, Teutonic chieftains, Chinese and Zulus, with not a thousandth of our culture. Arma virumque cano. I know all of Virgil by heart.

PYRAMUS. Mehnin aeide thea, and I, Homer!

ACHILLES. From every point of view, the times about to begin will be frightful.

PYRAMUS. Yes, the darkness of the Middle Ages. Without wishing to be a pessimist, I say mankind will never recover from the present catastrophe.

(ROMULUS *enters, wearing the imperial toga and wreath.*)

ACHILLES AND PYRAMUS. Hail Caesar!

ROMULUS. Hail: I am late. Yesterday's unexpectedly large number of audiences exhausted me. This morning I was so sleepy I was hardly able to climb over the athlete still snoring in front of my bed. Last night I governed more than at any time in all the twenty years of my reign.

ACHILLES. True, my Emperor.

ROMULUS. How strangely quiet it is here this morning. How desolate! Has everyone deserted?

(*Silence.*)

ROMULUS. Where is my daughter, Rea?

(*Silence.*)

ACHILLES. The Princess ...

PYRAMUS. And Emilian ...

ACHILLES. And the Empress ...

PYRAMUS. The Secretary of State, the Imperial Marshal, the cook and all the others ...

ROMULUS. Well?

ACHILLES. Drowned on their raft crossing to Sicily.

PYRAMUS. A fisherman brought the news.

ACHILLES. Only Zeno the Isaurian, together with his chamberlains, escaped on the ferry to Alexandria.

(*Silence.*)

ROMULUS. My daughter, Rea, and my son, Emilian.

(*He looks closely at the two chamberlains.*)

ROMULUS. I have no tears and I see none in your eyes.

ACHILLES. We are old.

ROMULUS. And I will die today. The Teutons will kill me. Yes, today. No pain can hurt me now. He who is about to die weeps not for the dead. Never was I more composed. Never more cheerful than now, when it is all over. My morning repast.

PYRAMUS. Your breakfast?

ACHILLES. But the Teutons, Your Majesty. At any moment the Teutons might –

PYRAMUS. And with all the flags in the empire at half-mast –

ROMULUS. Nonsense. There is no more empire to mourn and I shall make my exit as I have lived.

PYRAMUS. Very well, my Emperor.

(ROMULUS *sits down on an easy chair standing in the middle of the foreground.* PYRAMUS *brings a small table to him, laden with the* EMPEROR'*s usual breakfast. The* EMPEROR *looks contemplatively at the breakfast dishes.*)

ROMULUS. Why do you serve my last morning meal on this cheap tin plate and this cracked bowl?

PYRAMUS. The Empress took the imperial set of plates away with her. They belonged to her father.

ACHILLES. And now they are at the bottom of the sea.

ROMULUS. Never mind. Indeed, perhaps these old dishes are more fitting for my last meal.

(*He opens a soft-boiled egg.*)

ROMULUS. Augustus, of course, didn't lay again.

(PYRAMUS *looks at* ACHILLES, *pleading for help.*)

PYRAMUS. Nothing, my Emperor.

ROMULUS. Tiberius?

PYRAMUS. Julian, nothing.

ROMULUS. Flavian?

PYRAMUS. Domitian. But Your Majesty expressly did not wish to consume her products.

ROMULUS. Then just who laid this egg? (*He spoons out the egg.*)

PYRAMUS. Marcus Aurelius, as always.

ROMULUS. Anyone else lay?

PYRAMUS. Odoaker.

(*He is somewhat embarrassed.*)

ROMULUS. I declare.

PYRAMUS. Three eggs, Your Majesty.

ROMULUS. Mark my word! Today that one will lay a record.

(*The* EMPEROR *drinks his milk.*)

ROMULUS. You are both so solemn. What's on your minds?

ACHILLES. For twenty years we have served Your Majesty.

PYRAMUS. And for forty years before that we served Your Majesty's ten predecessors.

ACHILLES. For sixty years we accepted the direst poverty to serve our Emperors.

PYRAMUS. Every hackman was paid better than the imperial chamberlains. Let it be said openly this once, Your Majesty.

ROMULUS. True, true. However, you must remember that a hackney driver takes in more than an emperor.

(PYRAMUS *looks at* ACHILLES, *pleading for help.*)

ACHILLES. Caesar Rupf, the industrialist, offered us positions as valets in his house in Rome.

PYRAMUS. Four thousand sesterces a year and three evenings off a week.

ACHILLES. Time enough to write our memoirs.

ROMULUS. A fantastic offer. You are free to go.

(*He takes the imperial wreath off his brow and gives each a leaf.*)

Here, the last two leaves off my wreath. This marks the last financial transaction of my reign.

(*Battle noises are heard.*)

What is that noise?

ACHILLES. The Teutons, my Emperor. The Teutons are here!

ROMULUS. Why, then, I will just have to receive them.

PYRAMUS. Does Your Majesty wish to put on the imperial sword?

ROMULUS. But I thought it was pawned!

(PYRAMUS *looks pleadingly at* ACHILLES.)

ACHILLES. No pawnshop would take it. It is rusty, and Your Majesty had plucked out the imperial jewels a long time ago.

PYRAMUS. Shall I bring it?

ROMULUS. Imperial swords, my dear Pyramus, are best left in their corners.

PYRAMUS. Has Your Majesty finished breakfast?

ROMULUS. A little more asparagus wine, if you please.

(PYRAMUS *pours with a shaking hand.*)

ROMULUS. You both may go now. Your Emperor no longer has need of you. You were always faultless chamberlains.

(*The two chamberlains go off frightened. The* EMPEROR *drinks his glass of asparagus wine. A* TEUTON *enters from the left. He moves about freely and unconcerned. He is quite sure of himself and there is nothing about him except his trousers that is barbarian. He looks at the room as if he were walking through a museum, and indeed, makes notes now and then on a small pad, which he takes out of a leather briefcase. He is wearing trousers, a loose-fitting coat, broad-brimmed travel hat, all of it very unwarlike except for the sword at his side. Behind him comes a young man, wearing a war-like uniform which, however, must not be 'operatic'. The* TEUTON *notices, as if incidentally and among other objects, the* EMPEROR. *They look at each other with astonishment.*)

TEUTON. A Roman!

ROMULUS. Greetings unto you.

(*The young* TEUTON *draws his sword.*)

YOUNG WARRIOR (THEODORIC). Die, Roman dog!

TEUTON. Sheathe your sword, dear Nephew.

YOUNG WARRIOR. As you say, dear Uncle.

TEUTON. I beg your pardon, Roman.

ROMULUS. But, of course. You are a real Teuton, aren't you? (*He looks at him dubiously.*)

TEUTON. Of ancient lineage.

ROMULUS. I find it hard to imagine: Tacitus describes you people as having huge barbarian bodies, defiant cold blue eyes and reddish hair. But when I look at you, I would easily take you for a disguised Byzantine botanist.

TEUTON. My notions of what you Romans were like were quite

different, too. I had always heard of their bravery, but you were the only one who didn't run away.

ROMULUS. Obviously our ideas about different races and peoples are quite wrong. I suppose those are trousers covering your legs?

TEUTON. Of course.

ROMULUS. A truly remarkable garment. Where do you button it?

TEUTON. In front.

ROMULUS. Most practical.

(*He drinks more asparagus wine.*)

TEUTON. What are you drinking?

ROMULUS. Asparagus wine.

TEUTON. May I have a taste?

ROMULUS. I grew it myself.

(*The* EMPEROR *fills a cup. The* TEUTON *drinks and shudders.*)

TEUTON. Impossible stuff! Soon nobody will drink it. Beer is better.

(*The* TEUTON *sits down at the table next to* ROMULUS *and takes off his hat.*)

I must congratulate you on the Venus standing by the pond in your park.

ROMULUS. Why, is she something special?

TEUTON. A genuine Praxiteles.

ROMULUS. What bad luck! I always believed it was a worthless copy and now the antique dealer has already left.

TEUTON. Permit me.

(*With professional eye, he examines the shell of the egg the* EMPEROR *has eaten.*)

TEUTON. Not bad.

ROMULUS. Are you a chicken fancier?

TEUTON. A very keen one.

ROMULUS. Remarkable! I, too, am a chicken fancier!

TEUTON. You, too?

ROMULUS. Yes, I, too.

TEUTON. At last a human being with whom I can talk about my passion. Do the chickens in the park belong to you?

ROMULUS. Yes. A fine domestic breed. Imported from Gaul.

TEUTON. Do they lay well?

ROMULUS. Why, what do you think?

TEUTON. Be honest now. Judging by this egg they're only average.

ROMULUS. You're right. They are laying less and less. Confidentially, between us chicken fanciers, they worry me. Only one hen is really good.

TEUTON. The grey one with the yellow spots?

ROMULUS. How did you know?

TEUTON. Because I had this hen brought down to Italy. I wanted to know how she would fare in a southern climate.

ROMULUS. Now it is my turn to congratulate you. Truly, an excellent breed.

TEUTON. I developed it myself.

ROMULUS. You seem to be a first-rate chicken breeder.

TEUTON. As the father of my country, it is part of my job.

ROMULUS. The father of your country? Who are you?

TEUTON. Odoaker, ruler of the Teutons.

ROMULUS. I am truly pleased to make your acquaintance.

ODOAKER. And who are you?

ROMULUS. Romulus, Emperor of Rome.

ODOAKER. I, too, am pleased to make your acquaintance. Though, in fact, I knew right off to whom I was speaking.

ROMULUS. You knew it?

ODOAKER. Forgive the pretence. It is somewhat embarrassing for two enemies suddenly to find themselves face to face. That is why I thought it more useful at first to talk chickens rather than politics. May I present my nephew? Bow, Nephew.

YOUNG WARRIOR. Yes, dear Uncle.

ODOAKER. Please leave us, Nephew.

YOUNG WARRIOR. Very well, dear Uncle.

(*He goes off. Silence. The two look at each other.*)

ODOAKER. So you are Romulus. All these years my thoughts were always occupied with you.

ROMULUS. And you are Odoaker. I pictured you as my enemy – and now you are a chicken fancier just like me.

ODOAKER. Now the moment I waited for all these years has come.

(The EMPEROR *wipes his mouth with his napkin and rises.)*

ROMULUS. You find me ready.

ODOAKER. Ready for what?

ROMULUS. For death.

ODOAKER. You expected to die?

ROMULUS. The whole world knows how you Teutons deal with your prisoners.

ODOAKER. Have your thoughts about your enemies been so shallow, Emperor Romulus, that you must go by the world's judgment?

ROMULUS. What could you have in mind for me other than death?

ODOAKER. You shall see. Nephew!

(The YOUNG WARRIOR *enters from the right.)*

YOUNG WARRIOR. Yes, dear Uncle.

ODOAKER. Bow before the Emperor of Rome, Nephew.

YOUNG WARRIOR. Yes, dear Uncle.

(He bows.)

ODOAKER. Lower, Nephew.

YOUNG WARRIOR. Very well, dear Uncle.

ODOAKER. Throw yourself upon your knee before the Emperor of Rome.

YOUNG WARRIOR. As you say, dear Uncle.

(He throws himself upon his knee.)

ROMULUS. What does this mean?

ODOAKER. Now rise, Nephew.

YOUNG WARRIOR. Very well, dear Uncle.

ODOAKER. Now you may go again.

YOUNG WARRIOR. As you say, dear Uncle.

(He goes off.)

ROMULUS. I don't understand.

ODOAKER. I didn't come to kill you, Emperor of Rome. I came to subject myself and my entire people to you.

(ODOAKER, *too, kneels.* ROMULUS *is frightened to death.*)

ROMULUS. This is madness!

ODOAKER. A Teuton may be guided by reason, too, Emperor of Rome.

ROMULUS. You are mocking me.

(ODOAKER *rises.*)

ODOAKER. Romulus, a moment ago we talked sensibly about chickens. Isn't it possible to talk just as sensibly about nations and people?

ROMULUS. Speak.

ODOAKER. May I sit down again?

ROMULUS. Why do you ask? You are the victor.

ODOAKER. You're forgetting that just now I subjected myself to you.

(*Silence.*)

ROMULUS. Do sit down.

(*Both sit down,* ROMULUS *gloomily,* ODOAKER *watching* ROMULUS *carefully.*)

ODOAKER. You have seen my nephew. His name is Theodoric.

ROMULUS. Of course.

ODOAKER. A polite young man. 'Yes, dear Uncle; very well, dear Uncle,' all day long. His conduct is faultless. He is ruining my people with his way of life. He never touches girls, drinks nothing but water, and sleeps on the bare ground. Every day he practises with his weapons. Even now, while waiting in the ante-room, he is sure to be exercising.

ROMULUS. He is a hero, that is why.

ODOAKER. He is the ideal of the Teutons. He dreams of ruling the world and the people dream with him. That is why I had to undertake this campaign. I, all alone, opposed my nephew, the poets, and our public opinion, but I was forced to give in. I was hoping to conduct this war humanely. The opposition of the Romans was slight. Still, the farther south I advanced, the greater were the misdeeds of my army. Not because my army is any more cruel than any other army, but because *every* war turns men into beasts. I was shocked, I tried to call a halt to the campaign. I was ready to accept the sum offered by the manufacturer of trousers. Because up to now my captains could still be bribed, and because up to now I might still be able to have things my way. But only up to now. Soon I will not be able to do it any more. Then we shall have become, once and for all, a people of heroes. Save me, Romulus, you are my only hope.

ROMULUS. Your hope for what?

ODOAKER. For escaping with my life.

ROMULUS. Are you in danger?

ODOAKER. Right now my nephew is still tame; right now, he is still the polite young man. But one of these days, in a few years, he will kill me. I know this Teutonic loyalty.

ROMULUS. Is that why you wish to subject yourself to me?

ODOAKER. My entire life I have sought the true greatness of man, not that falsely acclaimed greatness of my nephew, who some day shall be called Theodoric the Great, if I know those historians. I am a peasant and I hate war. I sought a human way of life not to be found in the primeval Teutonic forests. I found it in you, Emperor Romulus. Your head steward, Ebius, saw through you.

ROMULUS. Ebi? At my Court? On your orders?

ODOAKER. He was my spy, but he sent good reports: Of a true human being, of a just man, of you, Romulus.

ROMULUS. He sent you reports of a fool, Odoaker. My whole life was aimed at the day when the Roman Empire would collapse. I took it upon myself to be Rome's judge, because I was ready to die. I asked of my country this enormous sacrifice because I, myself, was willing to be sacrificed. By rendering my country defenceless, I allowed its blood to flow because my own blood was ready to be spilled. And now I am to live; my sacrifice is not being accepted. Now I am to be the one who alone was saved. Even worse, just before you came I received the news that my only daughter, whom I loved, died together with her bridegroom, with my wife and the entire Court. I bore this news easily because I thought I was going to die. But now it hits me pitilessly and pitilessly proves me wrong. All I have done has become absurd. Kill me, Odoaker.

(*Silence.*)

ODOAKER. You are speaking in anguish. Conquer your grief and accept my submission.

ROMULUS. You are afraid. Conquer your fear and kill me.

(*Silence.*)

ODOAKER. You thought of your own people, Romulus, but now you must think of your enemies. If you do not accept my submission, if you and I do not make our way together, then the world will fall to my nephew; then a second Rome will rise, a Teutonic empire, as transitory as Rome and as bloody. If that comes to pass your work, the fall of Rome, will become absurd. You cannot escape your own greatness, Romulus. You are the only man who knows how to rule this world. Be merciful, accept my submission, become our Emperor. Protect us from Theodoric's bloody greatness.

(*Silence.*)

ROMULUS. I can do so no more, Odoaker. Even if I wanted to. You've taken from me the very thing that justified my actions.

ODOAKER. Is this your last word?

(ROMULUS *kneels.*)

ROMULUS. Kill me! I beg you on my knees.

ODOAKER. I cannot force you to help us. This is a misfortune for us. But neither can I kill you. For I love you.

ROMULUS. If you will not kill me, there is still a solution. The only man who would still murder me is sleeping in front of my bed. I will go and wake him.

(*As he rises,* ODOAKER *rises also.*)

ODOAKER. That is no solution, Romulus. You are desperate now.

Your death would be senseless. It would only make sense if the world were as you imagine it. But it isn't. Your enemy, too, is a human being who would do what is right, just as you do. You must accept your destiny. There is no other way.

(*Silence.*)

ROMULUS. Shall we sit down?

ODOAKER. What else can we do?

ROMULUS. What are you planning to do with me now?

ODOAKER. I will send you into retirement.

ROMULUS. Into retirement?

ODOAKER. It is the only possibility left to us.

(*Silence.*)

ROMULUS. Of all possible fates, retirement is the worst.

ODOAKER. Do not forget that I, too, am about to face the worst. You will have to proclaim me King of Italy. But it will be the beginning of my end unless I act promptly, here and now. Whether I want to or not, I will have to begin my reign with a murder.

(*He draws his sword and starts to go off to the right.*)

ROMULUS. What are you going to do?

ODOAKER. Kill my nephew. Right now I am still stronger than he.

ROMULUS. Now you are desperate, Odoaker. If you kill your nephew a thousand new Theodorics will rise. Your people feel differently about things than you do. Your people want the heroic life. You cannot change that.

(*Silence.*)

ODOAKER. Let us sit down again. We are caught in a vicious circle.

(*They sit down again.*)

ROMULUS. My dear Odoaker, I wanted to make my destiny and you wanted to avoid yours. Now it is our destiny to be politicians who have foundered on the rock of events. We thought we could drop the world from our hands, you, your

Germania and I, my Rome. Now we must busy ourselves with the pieces that are left. I wanted Rome's end because I feared its past; and you, you wanted the end of Germania because you shuddered at its future. Two spectres ruled us, for we have power neither over what was nor over what will be. Our only power is over the present. But we did not think of the present and now we founder on it. I must now live through the present in retirement, and weighing on my conscience will be a daughter I loved, a son, a wife, and indeed many other unhappy human beings.

ODOAKER. And I shall have to reign.

ROMULUS. Reality has put our ideas right.

ODOAKER. Bitterly right.

ROMULUS. Let us bear this bitterness. Let's try to endow the nonsense with sense! Try in the few years which will still be yours to rule the world faithfully. Give peace to the Teutons and to the Romans alike. To your task then, Ruler of the Teutons. Take up your reign! Maybe there will be a few years which world history will forget because they will be unheroic years – but they will be among the happiest this confused world has ever lived through.

ODOAKER. And then I shall have to die.

ROMULUS. Take comfort. Your nephew will kill me, too. He will never forgive me for having had to kneel before me.

ODOAKER. Then let us do our sad duty.

ROMULUS. Let us do it quickly. Once more and for the last time, let us play this comedy. Let us act *as if* final accounts were settled here on earth, as if the spirit won over the material called man.

ODOAKER. Nephew.

(*The nephew enters from the right.*)

THEODORIC. Yes, dear Uncle?

ODOAKER. Call in our captains, Nephew.

THEODORIC. Yes, dear Uncle.

(*He again goes off to the right. The room fills up with* TEUTONS, *dirty and fatigued from their long marches. They are dressed in monotonous linen clothes and simple helmets.* ODOAKER *rises.)*

ODOAKER. Teutons! Covered with dust and tired from your long marches, burned by the sun, you have now come to the end of your campaign. You are standing before the Emperor of Rome. Show him all honours.

(*The* TEUTONS *stand at attention.*)

Teutons! You have laughed at this man and mocked him in the songs you sang all day on the highways and at night by your campfires. But I discovered his humanity. Never have I seen a greater human being, and never shall you see a greater one, no matter who my successor is. Speak now, O Emperor of Rome.

ROMULUS. The Emperor is dissolving his Empire. Look, all of you, once more upon this tinted globe, this dream of a great empire, floating in space, driven by the slightest breath of my lips. Yes, look once more upon these far-flung lands encircling the blue sea with its dancing dolphins, these rich provinces golden with wheat, these teeming cities overflowing with life; yes, this empire once was a sun warming mankind, but at its zenith it scorched the world; now it is a harmless bubble and in the hands of the Emperor it dissolves into nothing.

(*Solemn silence. The* TEUTONS *stare in amazement at the* EMPEROR *who rises.*)

ROMULUS. I now proclaim Odoaker, Ruler of the Teutons, King of Italy!

TEUTONS. Long live the King of Italy!

ODOAKER. I, for my part, assign to the Emperor of Rome the villa of Lucullus in the Campania. Furthermore, he is to receive a yearly pension of six thousand gold coins.

ROMULUS. The Emperor's years of hunger are over. Take this wreath and the imperial toga. You will find the imperial sword among the garden tools. Will someone fetch me my namesake off the wall, the bust of King Romulus, the founder of Rome?

(*A Teuton brings him the bust.*)

ROMULUS. My thanks to you.

(*He puts the bust under his arm.*)

ROMULUS. Now I shall leave you, Ruler of the Teutons. I'm going into retirement.

TEUTONS. Long live Romulus the Great.

(SPURIUS TITUS MAMMA, *carrying a drawn sword, bursts in from behind.*)

SPURIUS TITUS MAMMA. Where is the Emperor? I shall kill him.

(*The* KING OF ITALY *steps up to him with dignity.*)

ODOAKER. Put down your sword, Captain. There is no emperor any more.

SPURIUS TITUS MAMMA. The empire?

ODOAKER. Is dissolved.

SPURIUS TITUS MAMMA. Then the last imperial officer slept right through the fall of his homeland.

(SPURIUS TITUS MAMMA *sinks down upon the Emperor's seat, downcast and broken-hearted.*)

ROMULUS. Gentlemen, the Roman Empire has ceased to exist.

(*The* EMPEROR *goes off slowly with bent head, carrying the bust under his arm. The* TEUTONS *stand by respectfully.*)

NOTES

Here is a difficult comedy, because it is seemingly a light one! Now what is the devotee of German literature to make of that? Style is what sounds solemn. Such a one will think of *Romulus* as a kind of farce, and will place it somewhere between Theo Lingen and Shaw. Nor is that fate entirely unfitting for Romulus. For twenty years he played the fool, and the world around him did not realize there was a method to his nonsense. That itself is something to think about! My characters must emerge from the way they appear. This applies to the actors and the director. Practically speaking: what should Emilian be like? He has been on the road for days, perhaps weeks, along secret paths, past destroyed cities, and finally he reaches the Emperor's villa which, after all, he knows well. But he asks now: is this the Emperor's villa in Campania? If we do not feel his unbelievable astonishment at seeing the Emperor's villa so dilapidated and looking like a chicken yard, then the question will seem merely rhetorical; this also holds when he asks his beloved, with fear and hesitancy: who are you? For truly, he no longer knows her. Truly he has forgotten her, but still he suspects that he once knew and loved this girl. Emilian is the counterpart to Romulus. His fate must be seen with human eyes, with the eyes, as it were, of the Emperor. For the Emperor can see behind Emilian's façade of the dishonoured officer, 'the victim of power, defiled a thousand times'. Romulus takes Emilian seriously, knowing him to be a human being who was captured and tortured, and who is unhappy. What Romulus will not accept is Emilian's demand that his beloved 'get a knife', nor will Romulus accept that Emilian should couple off his own beloved to save the country. If an actor does not discover the humanity within each of my characters, he cannot represent any of them. This holds for all my plays. But there is an additional difficulty facing the actor playing Romulus, and it is clearly this: he must not allow the audience to feel sympathetic towards Romulus too quickly. That is easily said and perhaps almost impossible to achieve. Still it should be clearly kept in mind as a tactical approach. What the Emperor really stands for should only be revealed in the third Act. In the first Act it should be quite understandable why the Captain of the Cavalry calls him 'a disgrace to Rome'; just as understandable should be Emilian's verdict at the end of Act Two, 'Down with the Emperor.' If Romulus sits in judgment over the world in Act Three, the world sits in judgment over him in Act Four. Look closely at what kind of a human I have sketched here: surely, a witty man, a man at ease and humane, but in the last analysis, a human being who proceeds with the utmost firmness and lack of consideration for others, a man who does not shrink from demanding the same absoluteness of purpose from others. He is indeed a dangerous fellow, a man determined to die. That is the terror lying within this imperial chicken fancier, this judge of the world disguised as a fool. His tragedy lies in the comedy of his end; instead of a sacrificial death he has earned for himself retirement. But then – and this alone is what makes him great – he has the wisdom and the insight to accept his fate.